Royalties earned from the sale of this book are being donated by the author to help the work of the Daughters of Charity in the Lebanon

A FORTUNE FOUND

A Fortune Found

MARY, GOD'S PRICELESS GIFT TO US

Jean Miller
Daughter of Charity

Sheed & Ward
London

ISBN 0 7220 3570 5

Copyright © 1990 by Jean Miller

First published in 1990 by Sheed & Ward Ltd
2 Creechurch Lane, London EC3A 5AQ

Book production Bill Ireson
Filmset by Waveney Typesetters, Norwich
Printed and bound in Great Britain
by BPCC Wheatons Ltd, Exeter

*To my companions, the Daughters of Charity
of the Provincial House, Mill Hill,
who are so accepting, so tolerant and so supportive*

Contents

Long before the earth your name was Mary!
Born of all the love God had for men!
Fashioned by the Finger of God's Wisdom,
A burning sun within a world of sin!
In your heart the message was implanted:
A word of hope . . . a word of God for men!
Nourished by your prayer and in the Spirit
You gave birth to God in Bethlehem!
   So sing to the Lord with all your heart!
   Praise him, praise him today!
   The wonders He has done for you
   speak to me of his ways!
Through your heart a sword will pass in sorrow,
Opening a mother's love for men!
Showing us the courage of a Woman,
Standing with her son against all men!
In your life we see God's faithful servant
Confidence burns bright within your heart!
You have walked beneath the cloud of Knowing!
The hand of God Himself has touched your heart!
   So sing to the Lord with all your heart!
   Praise Him, praise Him today!
   The wonders He has done for you
   speak to me of His ways!

FRANK ANDERSEN, M.S.C.
The Wonders He Has Done For You[1]

God's Gift

CHAPTER ONE

Full of Grace

'Grace' means 'gift of God'. At least, in the spiritual context it has a lot to do with God-giftedness. God's gifts come in many ways but the highest of them are far above our expectations and imaginations and that is perhaps why they cause problems for us. We baulk at their very magnitude. They are not ordinary enough for us, too good to be true.

The great problem which Christians, all through the ages of Christianity, have worried and wrangled about, and stumbled over, is the dual nature of Jesus. He is God. He is a man. How could the greatness of God be contained within the limits of a man? How could a man possibly be God? This is a problem because it is a mystery. We are trying to understand something which is beyond our grasp and will only be fully revealed when we meet God face to face.

We are trying to understand something which is beyond the limits of our experience. I remember once being asked by a blind child, 'What is the difference between blue and green?' I was unable to answer. I was unable to convey any understanding of those colours to that child. To me the answer was simple, but the child would have had to receive sight to be able to appreciate the difference between blue and green. The day will come when time merges into eternity for us, the scales of human limitation will fall from our eyes, and the mysteries of God will be clear to us. In the meantime God's greatest gift to us, the Word of God becoming one of us, will always be a mystery, and perhaps a problem for us.

A problem also crops up when we try to think about Mary. She is another gift God has given us and is closely linked with the Jesus-gift. We try to understand how she is just a woman, a human being as ordinary as any one of us, and at the same time she is Mother of God. We try to think about her position both in the Church and in our own lives and we find that this duality that we see in Mary is part of the problem of the duality that exists in her son, so full understanding of Mary will also come only when we see God face to face.

This does not mean that we can't ponder these mysteries. The more we do so the deeper will be our insights into the gifts God has given us. One of these insights touches on how Mary reconciles, in one person, the simplicity and individuality of her personal womanhood, and her universality, embodying, as she does, the 'People of God' of the Old Testament as well as the 'People of God' – who are the Church – of the New Testament.

At a particular epoch in time Mary lived the life of a simple Jewish woman. She was human and no more. If we think of her like this we see her as a young girl, married to a craftsman, bearing a child and living the insignificant life of a villager in a remote corner of Galilee. We don't even know for certain where and when she was born, or where and when she died and was buried. There is controversy about all of this! At the same time she is the 'woman', present from the beginning of creation, 'mother of the living', 'Daughter of Zion', and stretching forward in her 'Mother Church' role until the end of time and on into eternity. If we consider her in this wider role we are easily disconcerted. To some she may immediately appear to be remote from us. The magnitude of her sphere seems over-whelming. We can't take it in. And then she is Mother of God! This makes the dimensions of her personality greater still!

Perhaps it was in a subconscious attempt to by-pass these problems that popular devotion resorted to a rather sentimental 'Mother Mary' relationship. There seems to have been little seeking to *know* Mary, but perhaps quite a lot of pandering to the 'child' that is in each one of us, clinging to the 'parent' that was sought in Mary. This kind of devotion easily became immature, to say the least. However, it did help a very great number of people so it was good in so far as it went but it certainly doesn't satisfy everyone nowadays.

The instinct to see Mary as 'Mother' was right. But it is all the rich doctrinal content of Mary's Motherhood of God that we must ponder prayerfully if we are to build a balanced relationship between Mary and ourselves. It is only on this basis that a meaningful devotion to Mary can be established.

To get this right we must also take into account the duality that exists within ourselves. We are human beings and, in our own nature, nothing more. But, by the plan of God, brought about by the death and resurrection of Jesus, we can become Children of God: 'To all who did accept him he gave power to become children of God' (John 1:12), sharing in the divine life of Jesus, the Word of God: 'Do you not realize that Jesus Christ is in you?' (2 Corinthians 13:5), thus having the right to Mary's motherhood too!

A glance at these three dualities – in Jesus, in Mary and in ourselves, will give us, if not an understanding of the mysteries involved, at least a broader view and grasp of their implications. We will see the linking role of Mary in our salvation history. Thus:

The *Word of God* became the *Man-God*, Jesus.

This was accomplished through a woman, Mary, who thus became *Mother of God*.

Jesus, in his manhood, enabled *human beings* to become 'Christified' that is to say, '*Children of God*'.

The aim of this book is to consider many of these points in greater detail, so that, pondering them, we may reach a credible and fulfilling relationship with this very extraordinary woman, Mary, who is, at the same time so very, very ordinary, accessible and loving.

CHAPTER TWO

Ragged Rocks

One day follows another and many are boringly the same as the day before. Then, all of a sudden, for no apparent reason at all, one day is different. It was one of those days. Or perhaps it was I who was different. Something, from those mysterious inner depths, stirred within me and prompted me to run off on my own.

I was five years old and living with my family on one of the smaller Bermudian islands. There was no danger of any kind about, which perhaps explains how I escaped my mother's watchful eye. I was supposed to be playing on the stretch of grass in front of the house, but ran off up the road towards the bridge which joined our island to the next.

I knew what was on the other side – a post office, a few small shops and, down to the right, the landing stage for ferries, but I had never crossed that bridge alone. Nobody was about, I was absolutely alone and the world seemed very big. For just a moment I hesitated, then, feeling very daring and just a tiny bit scared, I crossed the bridge. The distance between the two islands was only a matter of a few feet but, had I crossed the widest ocean to a foreign country, I couldn't have been further from home than I was at that moment.

Turning my back on the post office and shops, I slithered down the bank beside the bridge to the water's edge. Then following a little path, I went under the bridge and came out on the left-hand side onto a stretch of ragged coral rocks. I had never been there before. This was really the great unknown but I knew just what I was about. The setting was ideal. It was here that I would begin to seek my fortune.

'To seek a fortune' was a phrase I had learnt from the fairy-tale books my parents used to read to me. I knew that anyone worth their salt always set out to seek a fortune, but I hadn't an idea what 'a fortune' was. However, confident that if I saw one it would stand out so that I couldn't miss it, I began to poke about in the many holes and crannies in the rocks to see if I could find my fortune. All I found were a few shells, some seaweed, a small crab or two and some little pieces of driftwood.

I soon began to think that I wasn't getting anywhere and, perhaps, I would find my fortune somewhere else, another day. Besides, my security was getting shaky so far away from home. Hastily I retraced my steps, ran back across the bridge and, as fast as my legs would carry me, made for the familiar territory of home. I hadn't been missed and I didn't tell anyone where I had been.

Of course, there was no deep thought or planning behind this little escapade. It was just a childish prank, an asserting of a little indepedence. However, when considered, it is a striking example of how remarkably 'on the spot' children's thinking and behaviour can be. Without intending it, or realizing it, I had done all the right things.

First of all I set out early. The early bird catches the worm! How many people, I wonder, miss their 'fortune' because they start seeking it too late and, having run after a few too many will-'o-the-wisps, end up empty and disillusioned.

Secondly, I went alone. There are definitely some things we can only do alone, quite alone. No-one else can tell us where to go or what to seek, no-one else can show us the way to where our fortune lies.

It's true, I didn't know what I was looking for, but how often that is the case with any one of us. We don't know what our fortune will look like or where to look for it, so our search is often blind and futile. Some people think a fortune means a lot of money. Actually that has nothing to do with what I am calling 'a fortune'. In fact a lot of money is often the beginning of misfortune. Many people seek happiness where it can't be found, and end up burnt out, disappointed and bitter. It may take a long time to discern that our fortune is to be found only in God.

The next thing I did was to cross a bridge. More than that, I went under the bridge, that is to say, I went through a tunnel. If ever we are to find our fortunes there may be many bridges to cross, perhaps one that will take us to a far off land where we have never been before. In actual fact it may not be very far away, but a decision will have to be made, a step taken and a change accepted which will distance us from our familiar circumstances. Maybe we will have to be very daring to cross that bridge and it will take us quite into the unknown. There may also be tunnels to go through, periods of darkness without any light showing at the end, but if we keep on bravely we will come out into the sunlight in wide open spaces full of opportunity.

Even so the situation may not be very clear. It may just look like ragged rocks but, perhaps, there may be something waiting for us, if not in a hole or crevice, well, just round the corner, a little further on. If we do nothing about it we won't find out. The child-that-I-was very rightly set about looking, even though no fortune was to be found there just then. At least a start had been made.

When I got back I told nobody, nobody at all, about my adventure. I don't remember being afraid or feeling guilty, as if I had done something wrong. No, I think that for the first time I had made the discovery that, to be ourselves and to find our own way in life, there are times when we need space to be alone. There are times when we need to be able to stand on our own two feet and keep our own counsel. There are bridges that are our own bridges, tunnels that belong only to us, adventures that no-one can share. If we don't learn this we will never grow up, never be mature. I think that perhaps the day I grew out of babyhood, though, of course, I still had a very, very long way to go – and I hadn't found my fortune. At that point I hadn't found Mary.

One of the Old Testament images evoking Mary is the feminine figure 'Wisdom'. 'Happy the man who discovers Wisdom. ... gaining her is more rewarding than silver, more profitable than gold. She is beyond the price of pearls, nothing you could covet is her equal. ... Her ways are delightful ways, her paths lead to contentment. She is a tree of life for those who hold her fast, those who cling to her live happy lives' (Proverbs 3:13–18).

Those who discover Mary have found their fortune. 'For she is an inexhaustible treasure to men' (Wisdom 7:14). For through her we find Jesus. All through our lives we can discover and re-discover her more deeply for all our lives we are seeking our fortunes. Seen from above, our efforts at fortune seeking may appear very puny, not unlike those of a little child searching among the coral rocks – for what? We, like her, often do not know! When our quest is finally over, our bridges, tunnels and the roughness of our rocks will appear puny too. In the meantime they are very real and often very terrifying. It is true that each one of us must make our journey alone, but we don't feel so alone if we are aware of the presence of Mary. Also, such is our human solidarity, we can help one another in our searching and this can be a great support. So, come with me then. Let's seek our fortunes, let's seek Mary!

CHAPTER THREE

Orange Blossom

My window gave onto our large back garden, a Lebanese garden, an orange grove. The beautiful golden fruit had not yet appeared, that would come later, nearer Christmas time, the time when the Son of God appeared upon our earth. Even the little dark green, marble-like baby oranges were not yet to be seen. The trees were in bloom, the fruit heralded by the heavy-scented, ivory-coloured blossom so popular at weddings. The flowers stood out against the shiny dark green of the foliage and the breeze wafted their perfume in through the open window of my room.

Over in the dispensary they would soon be distilling the blossoms to make orange-flower water. That would be sent to our hospital to help the patients to sleep. I breathed deeply and inhaled the heady perfume. Gradually I relaxed and felt a little drowsy. After dinner is a sleepy time anyway, and I was glad to let the perfume smooth away the stress and hassle of morning school. Before I had time to drop off to sleep completely the bell rang for afternoon classes. I picked up my satchel and set off, relaxed and ready for the fray.

Like the golden oranges, Christ appeared that first Christmas, 'When the fullness of time had come' (Galatians 4:4), but over the centuries his 'perfume' had been there before him inspiring hope and courage to an often stress-filled world. This 'perfume' is sometimes referred to as the 'Pre-existence' of Jesus. How can anyone pre-exist? – be there before they've actually come? Of course ordinary people can't. Before they are conceived they don't exist and can't be imagined.

Christ, as the man Jesus, didn't exist until the Angel Gabriel announced his coming and Mary conceived him in her womb (Luke 1:26–36). But it was the Son of God, the Word, who leapt down and became that little child: 'The Word was made flesh' (John 1:14), and 'The Word was God' (John 1:1). The Word, therefore, had always been, had always existed: 'In the beginning was the Word, the Word was with God and the Word was God' (John 1:1).

So, as God, the Word of God, Christ did exist before that first Christmas, had existed from all time and eternity. It is principally to this existence of the Word in time that we are referring when we speak of the pre-existence of Jesus, who was the Christ.

Jesus claimed this pre-existence for himself. He said: 'Before Abraham ever was I AM' (John 8:58). Abraham was the first truly historical personage of the Bible. The people spoken of before that were vague and legendary so that to say that he was – or, as he put it, IS – before Abraham, was equal to stating that he existed even in pre-historic times, that is, from all time, and in a divine way. 'I am who I am' (Exodus 3:14), was the answer God gave when Moses asked for God's name.

It is easier for us to understand the human existence of Jesus than this pre-existence of his, because, as a man, Jesus lived his human life as we live ours. His pre-existence is a spiritual thing, for God is spirit. Also it might almost be called poetic because of the language in which it is expressed in Scripture. You can't nail down poetry as you can prose, and you can't confine spirit within set limits as you can confine matter. That does not mean that poetry doesn't tell the truth, it does, but in beautiful, delicate, ethereal language, far more fitting to the truths it portrays than more hum-drum, matter-of-fact expression would be.

The Bible is full of poetic language. It has to be as it is speaking of spiritual truths; subtle, lofty, eternal themes – the thoughts of God.

One of these God-thoughts is the Wisdom theme. As dawn is breaking over creation we catch half glimpses of an elusive

10

figure flitting through the early morning mist. Now and then we catch sight of her in the glow of the new-born sunbeams and then she is gone again. What is 'Wisdom'? Do we really know? The question might better have been put as, 'Who is "Wisdom"?' rather than 'what'. St Paul said that he preached 'Christ, the power and Wisdom of God' (1 Corinthians 1:24). To Paul then, the Wisdom of God was Christ, and this mysterious figure, Wisdom, that we hear about in the Wisdom literature of the Bible, is surely no other than the personification of the pre-existence of Jesus, the Word and Wisdom of God.

But the 'Wisdom' spoken of in the Bible was a feminine figure, and was created: 'I, Wisdom, am *mistress* of discretion' (Proverbs 8:12), Yahweh *created* me when his purpose first unfolded' (Proverbs 8:22), whereas the Word was uncreated Godself. Who then is Wisdom? 'She is a breath of the power of God ... She is a reflection of eternal light ... image of his goodness' (Wisdom 7:25–26). 'With you (God) is Wisdom,' says the Sage, 'She knows your works, she was present with you when you made the world, she understands what is pleasing in your eyes' (Wisdom 9:9). Can we put a name to Wisdom? No, not really but 'Wisdom is a spirit, a friend of man' (Wisdom 1:6). 'I prayed,' said Solomon, '... and the spirit of Wisdom came to me' (Wisdom 7:7).

If we can't quite put a name to this elusive, feminine figure of Wisdom, perhaps we can catch a whispered hint, a gentle promise, a foreshadowing of a woman who would become the mother of 'He who is to come' (Matthew 11:3), he who would be eternal Wisdom in person. A woman, who was so closely and so intimately united with her son that, where Jesus is, the presence of Mary is always just perceptible. 'Her closeness with God lends lustre to her noble birth, since the Lord of all has loved her' (Wisdom 8:3). Perhaps that closeness of this woman to God applies even to the pre-existence of Jesus and his mother.

Be that as it may, to me the mysterious figure of Wisdom speaks of the all-time presence of both Jesus and Mary in creation. 'In the mystery of Christ she (Mary) is present even before the creation of the world'.[2]

It might be well just now, to clear up an objection or two. Though I am closely linking Jesus and Mary I am definitely not putting them both on the same footing. Jesus is God as well as man. Mary is no more than woman. Jesus we adore because he is God. Mary we honour as his mother, but we do not offer her the worship of adoration. Any honour we pay to Jesus is his by right. Any honour we pay to Mary is reflected honour really paid to God whose masterpiece she is. 'She is a breath of the power of God ... pure emanation of the glory of the Almighty ... She is reflection of eternal light' (Wisdom 7:26).

Jesus 'fills the whole creation' (Ephesians 1:23), and that, not only from the time of his birth in Bethlehem, but from all time, even from the beginning of the world. He always has been present, even when, as now, not visible to human eyes. This was first of all in virtue of his union with the Word of God, and secondly in virtue of his resurrection.

At his resurrection Jesus entered a different mode of being. From that moment even his body was in eternity. Eternity does not function like time but is a perpetual 'now'. So Jesus is now timeless, that is to say that he is not bound by time, any more than by place – he not only is, but always has been and always will be present everywhere in creation and at every moment of what we call time. This gives a fuller and deeper meaning to the form of his presence that I am calling his 'pre-existence'. It is not possible that he who 'fills the whole creation' should have been, at any time absent from the lives of human beings, those human beings of whom he is the saviour.

To some extent this must be true of Mary too, owing to the closeness of her union with her son and with his mission in the world. So, to sum up, I will say that Jesus, in one form or another, has been present in the world from its very beginning. And, in the same way as the moon reflects the light of the sun although it has none of its own, so Mary has also been present in some subtle, whispered way. 'She is the reflection of eternal

12

light' (Wisdom 7:26). I just can't think of a world entirely devoid of the feminine influence of Wisdom. Or was it Mary?

Is Mary, then, an elusive person we can't quite pin down, and about whom we know very little? No. It is true the facts we have of her human life are so meagre, her recorded words are so few, that we may think she is elusive, or else be tempted to try to fill in the gaps with surmisings and imaginings. To do this would serve no purpose, we have quite enough facts about her life on earth to know that she was a real woman, an ordinary woman, a wife and a mother and that she was a brave, strong and caring person.

If we try to wrap Mary up in the endless mundane details of a localized human life we will miss her universality and her availability to all. To reconstruct her human life in all those details might erect barriers, so great are the differences of culture, mentality, ways of life and thought, attitudes and so on, of people of different ages and in different parts of the world. The great majority of men and women scattered throughout the geography and history of the world, would, perhaps, not be able to identify with or relate to, a woman so closely knit to her own time and environment. A detailed life of Mary could possibly shut her out of the lives of all but a few, whereas her mission is to each one of us individually and personally, whoever we may be and whatever our circumstances.

We have recognized Mary's elusive, pre-figuring presence from the very creation of the world. We know that she lived a human life as any other woman, in a village nearly 2,000 years ago, and we realize that in becoming mother of Jesus she was united eternally to her divine son. We praise and thank God for this universality of Mary which enables her to step out of timelessness into each of our individual lives, meet us where we are, and adapt herself perfectly to our present needs and situations.

CHAPTER FOUR

Family Tree

Many of us know very little about our family tree, some nothing at all. Others can point to a long ascending list of names. It doesn't make much difference actually because none of us really know a lot about these people whose names figure on our family trees. In any case it's usually the father's line that is traced back from son to father. The mother, of course, also has a family tree and as we each have four grandparents and eight great-grandparents and so on, it is really dozens of family trees we would need to know if we want to find out who we are descended from.

Turning this over in my mind I wondered if there are any famous people in my ancestry, great people, heroes or saints! I should be very proud if I discovered that there were. On the other hand, if I found that I was descended from some notorious criminals I should probably sing in a rather lower key. Then, of course, an ancestor doesn't need to be notorious to be a criminal. Many highly respectable, or at least respected, people are hidden criminals. I mean their fraud, corruption, embezzlement or other evil ways have never been found out and are camouflaged under the best of appearances. Things being as they are, I may have had queer folks of all kinds in my ancestry if only I knew it. I expect, hopefully, there were also some fine, good, kind, upright and holy people among my forebears just as there were probably rascals. Mercifully I am, like every person, an entirely unique, new creation, but all the same, the blood of all these good, bad and indifferent people, who went before me, is mingled in my veins and has fashioned every aspect of my being: physical features, temperament, character, likes and dislikes, mannerisms and so on. There is therefore a solidarity between them and me that I cannot break. I am identified with my own. That is perhaps why history is so fascinating and why, when I read it, such passions as pride, shame, triumph, anger rise within me, all on account of deeds for which I am in no way personally responsible. It is just that I belong to these people.

Mary didn't drop from Heaven ready-made either. She also belonged to a 'People'. She was the product of the People of God, that 'Chosen People', sons and daughters of Abraham. They had gone before her with all their hope in the Promise, all their infidelities, all their repentance and mended faith. None of this in any way tarnished her spotlessness or lessened the beauty or newness of the unique purity of her personal creation. For hers was a special creation, not just a new creation, as is each of ours. We come into the world, so to speak, shop-soiled remnants of original sin, but Mary was brand new, purpose built to be the mother of the Word of God. Still she was in every respect a Daughter of Zion. Or rather she was *the* Daughter of Zion. In the Old Testament this title meant the personification of the People of God, the People of the Promise. This Mary was, it was through her that the Promise was fulfilled, for she it was upon whom the Spirit would descend so that she would conceive and bring forth the Word, the King of the Universe: 'Rejoice heart and soul, Daughter of Zion. Shout with gladness Daughter of Jerusalem. See now your King comes to you ...' (Zechariah 9:9).

There are traditions, but we don't really know for certain where Mary was born. We don't know for sure where she died. We don't know many details of her life. We have no portrait of her. But, as Daughter of Zion, we know her very well. She personifies a people. A people who, through thick and thin, believed and trusted in Yahweh and longed for the coming of the Promised One. A very human people who toiled and fought, who suffered and loved. A people capable of great heights of heroism and honour and goodness, and great depths of sin. People who feared and hoped, who rejoiced in the simple things

15

of life and called on God in their moments of despair. A people who were, well, just people, not so very unlike our own basic selves – the people we really are despite our twentieth-century-ness and our sophisticated modern technology.

Mary was in solidarity with all these people, her forebears, her people. She accepted them all, identified with them and represented them. She belonged to them and they belonged to her. The intervening years between the time of Abraham or earlier, and her own time didn't matter at all. Daughter of Zion she stood for them all, understood them and related to them in their history. Had they known it they could have related to her. Perhaps they did, through their aspirations and through the figures who foreshadowed her. Perhaps, through a certain intuition, they sensed her support, influence and love, in a veiled way, as their whole story was infused by her presence.

We already saw this when talking of her pre-existence, but it becomes clearer when we realize that all the longings and aspirations of her people were to culminate in her, Mary. Mary, 'Of her was born Jesus who is called the Christ' (Matthew 1:16). They named him 'Jesus' because he was 'the one who was to save his people from their sins' (Matthew 1:21). 'Salvation is from the Jews' (John 4:22). Yes, it certainly came from them. The whole mission of the Jewish People was to give the world its Saviour, but the woman who actually accomplished that mission in her own person was Mary, Daughter of Zion.

But her mission did not end there. In one sense it had only just begun. Christ came to establish a 'New Covenant' so that there would be a new People of God. This new people would be the assembly of all peoples who would accept Jesus as their Lord. This assembly we call the 'Church'. (The Greek for 'Church' is 'Ekklesia', a word meaning 'assembly'.) Jesus called it his Church and said that he would build it upon a rock (Matthew 16:18). This new people are the people of Christ's Church, 'By belonging to Christ you are the posterity of Abraham, the heirs he was promised' (Galatians 3:29). 'It is the children of the Promise who will count as the true descendants'

16

(Romans 9:8). So we, the new People of God are the latest generation in the family tree.

The family tree gets a bit exciting now. There are so many wonderful things that God wants to reveal to us that they come tumbling over one another in seeming confusion. What we are talking about are images, each one of which tells us something about the great truths of our faith, but they are only images, and it is the images, not the truths, that may be a little confusing.

Mary, we saw, is one with the People of God, so she is one with the Church. Yet in another way, she is Mother of the Church. How is that? Well, as Jesus, by his death and resurrection reconciled us to God and in so doing bestowed upon us a share of his own divine life (a gift we were destined to receive from the beginning, according to God's plan), we, the People of God, by this very gift, become one with Jesus. If we are one with Jesus, then we are children of Mary. So Mary is our Mother – that is she is Mother of the Church for we are the Church. As one of our race she is one with the Church, but spiritually she is Mother of the Church.

Looking at it from another angle we can say that the Church is our Mother and that we are children of the Church. In Ephesians 5, St Paul compares the relationship of Christ with the Church to the relationship of husband and wife in marriage, and some Scriptural commentators have seen 'the fruitful union of Adam and Eve as prefiguring the union of Christ and the Church'.[3] In this image, Mary, our mother, would identify with the Church in a model that we might call 'Mary Church'. This role fits Mary perfectly and links up with the concept of Mary as Daughter of Zion for 'all call Zion "Mother" since all were born in her' (Psalm 87 (86):5).

Yes, we were all born in her. It is true that she is one of us, a woman like any other woman, but she was a woman called to a tremendous mission, that of mothering the rest of us into supernatural life, and standing out as the model of our Mother-Church.

Sometimes we may get so caught up in these dazzling images

17

of Mary that we need to remind ourselves that she was a real woman. She was just an ordinary woman doing the daily chores, with time for laughter and time for tears. Like any other daughter of Eve she had her hopes and her fears, her joys and her pains, her moments of elation and moments of weariness and her times of deep sorrow.

I'm not trying to imply that Mary was just a little housewife. No, her 'career' was greater than any other woman's. I don't like the word 'career' though, it's hard and cold. Mary had a vocation and a mission the scope of which was immense, reaching far beyond the confines of her village or homeland, and this made her tower high above any other woman. But basically she was a woman.

What does being a woman mean? I think it means being open to life, to receive it, to nurture it, to bring it to birth and constantly to affirm it. Taken in its narrowest sense this means that woman was made for motherhood but, while extolling motherhood as the height of woman's glory, I would insist that a woman is much more than her sexuality or something biologically fitted for childbirth. Her motherhood itself is only understood in its full dignity if all woman's potentialities are developed and realized.

Life is the key word. Woman is open to receive it and affirm it. From the very beginning of time God set up the woman as the Life-giver in opposition to the Death-dealer, saying to the Evil One: 'I will make you enemies of each other, you and the woman, your offspring and her offspring. It will crush your head' (Genesis 3:15). This was rightly done as woman was to be 'the mother of all who live' (Genesis 3:20) and so must be open to life, not death. There are many ways of nurturing life and many ways of dealing death, but wherever there is spark of life, in no matter how unlikely surroundings or form, woman, true woman, is open to it, nurtures it, draws it out and affirms it.

The Life to which Mary was open and which she brought to birth was greater than all other life and that makes her greater than any other women, 'Of all women you are the most blessed'

(Luke 1:42). That Life was the Life of all life, the author of life, the Word of Godself who came to earth that we may have life: 'I have come that they may have life and have it to the full' (John 10:10). Mary was the gate through which Life came into the world, she was truly the new Eve, Mother of all those who live. She received this Life, brought it to birth and offers it to all the generations making up the human family tree, God's family tree. She is ever at hand affirming and nurturing that Life in us, her children, each one of whom she sees as an extension of her own divine Son, Jesus, and loves each one as her very own.

CHAPTER FIVE

Shop-soiled and Seconds

Walking through the big store, looking at the beautiful goods displayed, I was amazed to learn that they were all 'seconds', not one of them without some flaw or defect. I could hardly believe it. I picked up a pair of shoes. Surely, I thought, there is nothing wrong with these! Closer inspection, however, showed that the stitching on both sides didn't quite correspond. In another department were lovely china tea-sets, coffee pots and dinner services. None of them was quite perfect. And so it went on as I strolled from department to department: dresses, coats, underwear, bedding and furniture. The defects were hardly noticeable, would they really matter? Especially as everything was so inexpensive! And yet all the other stores in the town, the stores that sold only unflawed perfect articles, at very high prices, were all full of shoppers, and their sales were obviously in no way harmed by the competition from the 'seconds' store, in spite of its low prices.

The reason is clear. We don't like and don't want second best. (Though for practical purposes we may often have to opt for 'seconds', or shop at jumble sales.) We like to think, and to know, that the objects that become our possessions are perfect, neither flawed nor shop-soiled. It has something to do with our self image, our rightful pride or dignity. We feel it lowers us just a little to accept spoilt goods. That attitude is right.

I think that is God's attitude too. When God first created the world everything was perfect: 'God saw all that he had made, and indeed it was very good' (Genesis 1:31). And that was the way God intended things to stay. That is the way we, humankind, would have stayed if we had followed the maker's instructions; but we didn't and something went wrong.

The long and the short of it is that we all come into this world flawed. It is a spiritual flaw but its influences are far reaching and affect all aspects of our lives. Put it like this: we are all 'seconds'. Yes, it is true that we are God's handiwork and God's work is perfect, but somewhere along the production line contaminated material infiltrated. That was way back at the beginning of the history of the human race. The contamination is still there; although we can admire the many excellent qualities there are in men and women (after all, God did make us), the flaw is still there, which has a lot to do with there being so much wrong with the world today.

That is also why the Word of God came among us, not only as the high point of creation, but as the saviour of the human race. Jesus came to repair the damage done by original sin – that is, the contamination I have been speaking about.

Have there never been any exceptions to this state of everyone coming into the world flawed in some sort? Has the whole human race been tarnished in this way? Is there not *one* person who we could hold up as an example of what we were intended to be? This would help us from losing hope that one day we may find again our lost integrity, the perfection that was meant to be ours as children of God. Indeed there is. God didn't want us to be seconds, and when it came to choosing a mother for the Word of God, 'seconds' just wouldn't do. The Word of God was being sent to restore what had been contaminated and could not possibly be associated in this mission with anything however remotely tainted.

There was difficulty here. All human nature had been affected, all human nature needed purifying. (We call this purification 'redemption', which means buying back because a price was to be paid.) As Mary is one of us, solidly rooted in human nature, part of our family tree, she would also need redemption, yet it wasn't fitting that she should ever be contaminated.

21

God is never stuck for a means. God always achieves the end divinely planned from all eternity. Mary's redemption would not be a cure like ours, it would be a prevention. It was a redemption all the same, the price was paid, like ours was, by Jesus' death on the Cross.

That's how it was done, but what exactly is obtained by redemption? I said that human nature was flawed. That flaw prevents the flow of divine life into our souls. Without this divine life we are human beings and no more. God wasn't bound in justice to give us any more. But God had destined us to share eternal life with Godself. To make human nature compatible with eternal life something had to be added to human nature. That something is a share in God's own divine life. This does not make us gods but children of God, capable of entering the Trinitarian love-life which means everlasting happiness. The flaw blocked the inflow of divine life. So the first thing redemption does is to remove the flaw, then, with the inflow of divine life, divine son and daughtership is bestowed. The ordinary way of obtaining this is by baptism, though God, being God, can bestow divine life extra-sacramentally in ways we know nothing about.

Did you know that when you were baptized you received more than just a name? Do you realize that you became a child of God, living on a totally different level from just the human level, that you had been raised to a higher plane, living with the life of Godself?

Mary was, as I said, redeemed by prevention 'through the *foreseen* merits of Jesus Christ'.[4] The flaw never marred her, so from the very first moment of her existence she was filled with divine life; 'Hail full of grace!' (Luke 1:29).[5] This is what we call the 'Immaculate Conception'.

The Immaculate Conception of Mary was a unique privilege. No-one else comes into the world unflawed and filled with divine life; but it was not for her own sake, as something that she could enjoy for herself alone, that Mary was given this privilege, it was in view of her motherhood of Jesus that she was

22

immaculate, spotless. And Jesus was the Word of God made man who came to redeem us.

It is easy to think of the motherhood of Mary in connection with the Christmas story and so to picture Mary just as the mother of a lovely baby boy. That was true, but to look at it just like that is to take a very superficial view of a most profound mystery. Mary was the mother of our Redeemer. That was the point of her motherhood. Other mothers bear children who perhaps, later in life, *become* this or that, Jesus didn't *become* the Redeemer, he *came* as the Redeemer. So it was to the Redeemer that Mary gave birth. This surely coloured the whole of her motherhood. (In another chapter we shall look at this more closely.)

In the meantime we like to think of Mary as being open to Life, to him who is Life itself. That is an uplifting, a happy thought, but the thought of a redeemer makes us a little uneasy. It reminds us that we are shop-soiled and seconds, that there is something amiss with us and that we ourselves do wrong, that we *need* a redeemer. We would rather think that we didn't need anyone or anything, that we were all right as we are. If we won't face up honestly to the fact of our inherited sinfullness, to which we have added our own personal sins, we will miss out on redemption. Christ said, 'I did not come to call the virtuous but sinners' (Matthew 9:13), so if I am not a sinner (or consider that I am not) he didn't come for me. That's a frightening thought.

But if, admitting our sin, we accept our Redeemer, we are safe for, 'God in Christ was reconciling the world to himself, not holding man's faults against him' (2 Corinthians 5:18), and 'For anyone who is in Christ there is a new creation, the old creation has gone, and now the new creation is here' (2 Corinthians 5:17).

This new creation began in Mary who was the first of the redeemed. And as it was she who gave birth to him who was to save us all from sin and death, how grateful we should be to her, and how much we should love her!

What a great thing, also, it is for poor, battered, shop-soiled humankind to be able to look up to this one beautiful example of what creation was meant to be according to God's plan for us from the beginning, and to know that, low and all as we have fallen, the human race was not entirely submerged, there was one radiant exception. And we now have hope that we shall be lifted up again, and to what heights!

O Mary conceived without sin, pray for us who have recourse to you.

CHAPTER SIX

Servant and Son

The woman was introduced to me as 'Im-Saleem'. The little lad holding her hand was 'Saleem'. 'Im' means 'mother', so this was Saleem and his mother, in that order. I was in the Middle East at the time and Im-Saleem was coming to earn a little money in the workshop I was running. What her own name really was I found out eventually, but we never called her anything but 'In-Saleem'.

Since the birth of her first-born son Im-Saleem had in some way become identified with him. The important thing from then onwards was her motherhood of Saleem, so, for the rest of her life she would be known as 'Im-Saleem' – Mother-of-Saleem. It was the same with the other women in the workshop. We had 'Im-Yousef', 'Im-Fareed', 'Im-Tannous' and so on.

Every woman's life is transformed by the birth of a child. The joys, the sorrows, the failure or success of a child colour the life of a mother. She shares the fame, the wealth or the disgrace of her child. Once a mother, her life will never be the same again. Of no mother has this ever been more true than of Mary. It is certain that Mary was jolted into an entirely new existence, received a new identity at the birth of Jesus. She became the Mother-of-Jesus, that is to say of our Saviour, of our Redeemer.

There is little to be gained by surmising how much Mary realized, at any given moment, what her role signified, but it is safe to say that she must have been an intelligent woman, with an intelligence enlightened by prayer and the reading of Scripture. And we do know what the Scriptures would have told her. She knew from the Prophet Isaiah that 'the One who was to come', the Messiah, was also going to be the Suffering

25

Servant of Yahweh. This is spelt out by Isaiah in the four songs of the Servant of Yahweh (Isaiah 42:1–4 and 6–7, 49:1–6, 50:4–9, 52:13 to 53:12).

If we look a little closer at these four Servant songs we will not only understand Jesus rather better, but also have a deeper knowledge of Mary as she was so closely united to her Redeemer-Son that her whole life was entwined with his.

First of all let's clear up a seeming contradiction. The Angel told Mary, 'He will be great and will be called the Son of the Most High. The Lord God will give him the throne of his ancestor David' (Luke 1:32). How then did Isaiah speak of him as a suffering *servant* of Yahweh? Are we sure that this was the same person, Mary's son? Mary herself might have been a little perplexed. We know that at times she turned things around in her mind, she 'pondered' upon them (cf. Luke 2:19 and 50–51). But as Jesus grew to manhood and his public life advanced, his persecution and death loomed ever bigger and bigger on the horizon. Mary would have been able to see the Scripture scroll unrolling before her eyes and greater and greater would have become her realization that the suffering Servant of Yahweh was in fact her son.

However, for a long time I was puzzled, perhaps disconcerted would be a better word, by the title 'Servant' in these prophecies of Isaiah. Surely, I thought, the Messiah, the Promised Anointed One, the Saviour was Jesus, and Jesus is God. How then refer to him as a 'servant'. It didn't seem to fit. Even we don't use the word 'servant' much nowadays. Nobody wants to be a servant, it is considered demeaning. Actually a servant is only one who serves, and there is nothing more beautiful than the loving, selfless attitude of one who serves his or her fellow human beings: 'Just as the Son of Man came not to be served but to serve, and give his life as a ransom for many' (Matthew 20:28).

Besides, Jesus was, as Moses said he would be, 'from among yourselves, from your own brothers' (Deuteronomy 18:15). In other words, in his human nature he was a creature, and all creatures are, by definition, servants of God. As Word of God, Jesus was Lord of all. As a man he was a servant of Yahweh. And it was in this, his human nature that he suffered and redeemed us. He accepted this knowing well what he was about. He came to serve humankind by saving us.

'His state was divine (he was God), yet he did not cling to his equality with God but emptied himself to assume the nature of a slave and became as men are' (Philippians 2:6–7).[6]

It was of this special servant of God that Isaiah was talking. It was of this servant, also, that Gabriel was speaking when he told Mary that she would conceive a son and 'must name him Jesus (Saviour)' (Luke 1:32). Mary was quick on the uptake. She herself immediately identified with her servant-son, and her reply was: 'I am the handmaid of the Lord' (Luke 1:38).

There is an echo of this in the Psalms. We know that Jesus, as man, prayed the Psalms as every Jew did. We can almost hear him saying, 'Gladden the soul of thy servant, for to thee O Lord, do I lift up my soul ... give strength to thy servant and save the son of thy handmaid' (Psalm 86(85):4 and 16).[7]

To return to Isaiah and the four Servant songs. Let's see how his prophecy fits Jesus, and, indeed, was fulfilled by him.

Isaiah, speaking in the name of Yahweh, says: 'Here is my Servant ... my Chosen in whom my soul delights' (Isaiah 42:1). When Jesus was baptized by John a voice was heard from Heaven saying: 'This is my Son, the Beloved, my favour rests on him' (Matthew 3:17) and, on this occasion John himself confirms this saying: 'I have seen and I am the witness that he is the Chosen one of God' (John 1:34).

Yahweh determined the name of this 'Chosen One'. 'Yahweh called me before I was born. From my mother's womb he pronounced my name' (Isaiah 49:1). And the Angel said to Mary: 'You must name him Jesus' (Luke 1:32), a name which means 'Saviour' or 'The Lord is Salvation'.

The Holy Spirit was with this child, this child conceived by a virgin by the power of the Spirit overshadowing her. 'The maiden is with child and will soon give birth to an son' (Isaiah

7:14). 'I am a virgin,' said Mary. 'The Holy Spirit will come upon you and the power of the Most High will cover you with its shadow' replied the angel.

The Spirit's work did not end there: 'I have endowed him with my Spirit,' said God through Isaiah, 'that he may bring true justice to the nations' (Isaiah 42:1). Jesus was aware of this and, quoting Isaiah 61:1–2, he applied the prophecy to himself declaring: 'The Spirit of the Lord has been given to me, for he has anointed me. He has sent me to bring the Good News to the Poor' (Luke 4:18). That was Jesus' mission. 'I have appointed you as a covenant of the people and light to the nations' (Isaiah 42:6). Jesus, knowing the terms, accepted this mission. 'This is my blood, the blood of the Covenant, which is poured out for many for the forgiveness of sins' (Matthew 26:28). And Mary knew that it was her blood that flowed in his veins.

His calling was clear, his mission was clear: in the establishment of the New Covenant with the nations he would shed his blood. Suffering would be his lot on account of our sins. That comes across very clearly in the Servant songs: 'He was pierced through for our faults, crushed for our sins. On him lies a punishment that brings us peace and through his wounds we are healed' (Isaiah 53:5).

We are inclined to take our sins pretty lightly and can rationalize most of them. But, in reality, sin must be horrendous. This is brought home to us when we look at what God does to straighten out the mess we make. Even centuries before the Passion actually took place Isaiah foresaw it and said: 'Yahweh burdened him with the sins of us all ... Yes, he was torn away from the land of the living; for our faults struck down in death' (Isaiah 53:6 and 8). '... The crowds were appalled on seeing him ... so disfigured did he look that he seemed no longer human' (52:14) '... a thing despised and rejected by men, a man of sorrows and familiar with suffering' (53:3) '... and yet ours were the sufferings he bore, ours the sorrows he carried' (53:4). John confirms this: 'Pilate handed him over to them to be crucified ... after Jesus had taken the vinegar he said: "It is accomplished" and bowing his head he gave up the Spirit' (John 19:16 and 30), and all this '... though he had done no wrong' (Isaiah 53:9).

Mary had done no wrong yet she was involved in all this, so entwined was her life with Jesus, the weft and the warp interwoven as in one fabric. Simeon left her with no illusions when he met her in the Temple at the time of Jesus' presentation. Having recognized Jesus as the promised saviour he said: 'My eyes have seen the salvation which you have prepared for all the nations to see.' Then turning to Mary he added, 'And a sword will pierce your own soul' (Luke 2:30 and 35). That prophecy was certainly fulfilled on Calvary when 'near the cross of Jesus stood his mother' (John 19:25).

To judge from all the violence of which Jesus was the victim, anyone would have thought that it was with a man who was himself violent that the authorities were dealing, a dangerous revolutionary. On the contrary he was gentle, and fulfilling a mission. 'He does not cry out or shout aloud nor make his voice heard in the streets. He does not break the crushed reed or quench the wavering flame' (Isaiah 42:2–3). 'I have appointed you ... to open the eyes of the blind, to free captives from prison and those who live in darkness from the dungeon' (Isaiah 42:7).

So it is that all through the Gospel stories we see Jesus having compassion for people, helping and healing them. He himself said: 'I am the light of the world, anyone who follows me will not be walking in the dark; he will have the light of life' (John 8:12).

In the third Servant song we see the help God will give this servant-son. 'The Lord Yahweh comes to my help, so I am untouched by the insults ... My vindicator is here at hand' (Isaiah 50:7–8). And in the fourth song we hear of the vindication: 'His soul's anguish over he shall see light and be content ... I will grant whole hordes for his tribute ... for surrendering himself to death and letting himself be taken for a sinner while he was bearing the faults of many and praying all the time for sinners' (Isaiah 53:11–12). The 'hordes' who are his tribute are surely all those who accept the salvation which he won for us and offers to each one of us. 'A huge number, impossible to count from every nation, race, tribe and language' (Revelation 7:9).

He came to set captives free but we have to do something about it ourselves: 'Free your neck from its fetters, captive Daughter of Zion' (Isaiah 52:2). Mary, the Daughter of Zion *par excellence*, is sinless and so can't be fettered, except, in so far as we, who are her people, with whom she is in solidarity, remain captive. Certainly, shaking ourselves free from the fetters of sin and bad habits is not something we can do alone, but this text suggests that Mary is being instructed to help us, if only we will turn to her!

In a small book like this I have been able to deal only very briefly with the subject of Jesus' role as the Suffering Servant. It is a hard subject and one that we find it very difficult to come to terms with. We need to read these prophesies and the Gospels and ponder them with Mary. When reading the Gospels we are often perplexed, as were the disciples after the crucifixion of Jesus, a crucifixion that is re-enacted in the sufferings of the world about us and in our own lives. We need Jesus to explain things to us as he did to the two disciples on the way to Emmaus (even if he does so with a gentle reproach) 'You foolish men! So slow to believe the full message of the prophets! Was it not ordained that the Christ should suffer and so enter into his glory? Then, starting with Moses and going through all the prophets, he explained to them the passages throughout the Scriptures that were about himself' (Luke 24:26–27).

The two disciples then invited Jesus into their house and they recognized him in 'the breaking of bread'. We still 'break bread' as that is an expression that refers to the Eucharist. If we pray the Scriptures and recognize Jesus in the breaking of bread, we may be able to say like those two disciples: 'Did our hearts not burn within us as he talked to us on the road and explained the Scriptures?' (Luke 24:32). This will be most likely to happen in the company of Mary, as at the marriage feast at Cana when, 'the Mother of Jesus was there ... (and) ... he let his glory be seen, and his disciples believed in him' (John 2:1 and 11).

CHAPTER SEVEN

A Spark from Heaven

I know there are many people who are afraid of thunder and lightning. I know that lightning can kill. That is true also of a lot of natural phenomena. People drown in the sea, get lost in the snow and can be stung to death by bees. That does not prevent us seeing beyond the dangerous element in nature and learning something of the majesty, power, wisdom and love of God exemplified in natural phenomena.

Personally I love thunderstorms. When God makes a big noise like that in the sky I really know that a tremendously powerful God is all around me, and if I am just a little bit scared, I hold on tighter to Godself. There's a flash and, in an instant, a streak of white light rips down from heaven to earth and the silence of the night is shattered by a mighty crack of thunder. Humankind can do a lot of marvellous things but no-one, absolutely no-one can, by an act of willpower, call that thunderbolt down from heaven to earth. Only the power of God is behind the forces of nature that produce such astonishing manifestations.

So also, when the mighty Word of God sprang down from the Trinity into the womb of Mary, it was not the result of any human willing, any human action, but solely by the will and power of God. To make this absolutely clear, Jesus had no human father. It might be argued that Jesus could have had a human father; the manner of his coming would have made no difference to his being the Son of God, he was that by his very nature which nothing could change. But it wouldn't have been so clear to us that it was God's will and action alone, God's decisive intervention in the affairs of humankind, dictated by

God's loving care for us, that sent the Word descending like lightning into our midst. Not needing a human father would highlight the fact that God was Jesus' real father. So the mother of Jesus bore him in virginity. It is as well to understand this, otherwise the 'virgin birth' might be taken as a slur on marriage as if marriage wouldn't have been worthy of the birth of the man-God, as if virginity were a holier state than marriage. I don't think this is the case. Virginity and marriage cannot be compared and contrasted; they are two different states each with their own values. But when it came to the birth of Jesus there was no question of his being just the fruit of a human union, his birth was uniquely an act of God.

For Mary, her virginity meant a total openness to God, an unlimited receptivity involving her whole being. This signified a relationship with God that was so close that only perfect virginity was compatible with it. It meant an undistracted emptiness of all else. To be so entirely filled by God as Mary was required that space, a space that only virginity could ensure. All her other relationships revolved around this one super-relationship with God and what God wanted for her and of her. And what God wanted was that she should be the mother of Jesus, Jesus our redeemer.

Only a creature totally untainted by even the slightest suggestion of sin and sinfulness, could be crystal clear enough to sustain this openness and receptivity. Spotless and immaculate Mary was, God had seen to that, so she was able to be completely available.

To use our, limited, human language when speaking of God means that we will be inaccurate. But it is the best that we can do, so we might almost say that such a degree of receptivity as was Mary's, is irresistible to God. It, so to speak, drew God, so that with an inrush of divine life God filled the creature that was so open to Godself. So it was that Mary became pregnant with divinity.

The Trinity already indwelt her. The divine life already animated her soul. Already she lived by the love-life of the

Godhead. That had been granted her by the magnificent preventive redemption that was hers. The godliness within her called to the holiness of Godself. God invaded her whole being and united her to Godself, while the overshadowing of the Spirit gave her motherhood of the divine person, the Word of God who became man in the person of Jesus.

Mary's virginity remained intact, for all that her motherhood was real and human. Her womanhood also remained intact. She was not divinized, did not become God. She was in no way a goddess but was always a truly human woman, like one of ourselves, but so highly favoured! The originator of her motherhood, however, was divine as was the child she bore. Jesus was truly divine, that is to say, he was God while being, at the same time, a real true man, a human being among human beings, a creature like the rest of us in so far as his humanity was concerned.

This meant that Mary, daughter of Eve, Daughter of Zion was really mother of God. It is true that it was his humanity and not his divinity that he drew from her, but she was not the mother of half a person but of the whole person. She was mother of a person who was God as well as man.

That Mary should become the mother of Jesus in virginity is fairly widely accepted. Everyone knows that she was the mother of Jesus and she is commonly referred to as the 'Virgin Mary', but the question arises as to what happened after that. Did she always remain a virgin or did she become the mother of other children in the ordinary way?

Mary was married to Joseph so humanly speaking it would have been quite in order, and very natural, for her to have other children. The Gospels speak of Jesus as Mary's 'first born', 'she gave birth to a son, her first born' (Luke 2:7), and mention is also made of his brothers and sisters, '... His brothers James and Joseph and Jude ... His sisters too, are they not all here with us?' (Matthew 13:55–56).

Nothing is proved by these quotations. 'First born' only indicates that there were no previous children. As for the 'brothers and sisters', they were probably members of the extended family, cousins and other relations who, according to the custom and language of the East, are referred to as 'brothers' (cf. our use of 'brethren' in the expression 'dearly beloved brethren' commonly heard in our churches a few decades ago!)

Mary's relationship with God was unique. No other creature ever had, nor ever will have, such receptivity filled with such plenitude as Mary had. Never can creature be so closely united to the Creator as she was. Then how it can be imagined that Mary could ever have withdrawn any of that availability which was her virginity, that virginity that had been consecrated by her motherhood of Jesus? Her relationship with God was too close and too sacred to permit of an intimate, conjugal relationship with any man. Joseph's role was to protect her virginity and her honour.

Certainly Joseph would have understood this when the 'Angel of the Lord' appeared to him and informed him that, 'Mary has conceived what is in her by the Holy Spirit. She will give birth to a son and you must name him Jesus, because he is the one who is to save his people from their sins' (Matthew 1:20–21).

A revelation like that would have awed any man. Joseph would surely have been awed and honoured to the point of the most self-effacing humility as he took up his charge. He too would have been especially chosen by God, and must have been very open and receptive to have been able to offer his virginity to God in this way, as he stood in for God, filling the role of earthly father to the divine Word, God's Son.

As for Mary's 'other children', are they not ourselves, God's adopted sons and daughters, sisters and brothers of Jesus? Yes, we are most certainly the spiritual sons and daughters of Mary just as truly as Jesus was her son physically.

And, as true children, we must imitate our mother in her openness and receptivity to God. Whether in marriage or in celibacy all should share something of Mary's availability to

God. Humankind can do marvellous things, even reach the stars, but it can't call down eternal life. That life without which our eternity, yes even our life on earth for all its apparent progress and successes, is an empty, dismal failure. That wonderful gift of supernatural life only God can give. God wants to bestow it upon us, this was God's plan from the very beginning and before. We were created for that but we can't receive this great gift unless we are open and receptive to it. In this openness and receptivity we can, all of us, share in some degree in the virginity of Mary.

CHAPTER EIGHT

Just Round the Corner

The wings of the old mill on the hill over across the fields could just be seen again. The leaves on the trees, that all through the summer had hidden the mill from view, had turned orange and brown and now lay dead on the ground. Soon the snow would come and bury the dead. All signs of life, leaves and flowers and bird song would be gone leaving a chilly sense of loss.

It's not only nature that dies, there is death all around us: 'Five die in fire.' 'Eleven killed in motorway pile-up.' 'Bomb attack kills thirty four.' 'Floods drown over two hundred.' 'More than three thousand feared dead in earthquake.' There are millions wiped out in never-ending war and the old man across the road has had a heart attack. 'Parents grieving for their little girl found murdered' and, and, and ... People we know and people we don't know, strangers and those dear to us, the end is just the same and one day it will be our turn. All this sounds very gloomy but when the snow lies thick upon the ground we know that spring is just around the corner. And when blades of grass begin to show, we know that bird song and buds and blossom will soon follow. After the annual reminder of death there is the annual hope of resurrection.

Yes, resurrection is a fact. We know that because Jesus rose from the dead: 'God raised this man Jesus to life, and all of us are witnesses to that' (Acts 2:32).

Where does Mary come into all of this? According to the opinion of a few, Mary did not die. They hold that her death was only apparent, it was really only a kind of sleep, which, they say, explains the term 'dormition' – 'sleeping', which is applied to

Mary's death. These people hold that after such 'sleeping' Mary was carried up to Heaven. It is not the traditional teaching of the Church that Mary did not die. Karl Rahner voiced the Church's belief when he wrote: 'But it cannot be doubted that she did die'.[8]

Surely her very solidarity with us, the rest of the human race, demanded that she should share our lot? Knowing that she walked the same dark road that we must all walk, is much more helpful and supportive for us than the thought of her being exceptional and privileged. That would be out of keeping with all her other gifts, which she received *for us*.

The objectors say that it was because of her sinlessness that Mary was not subjected to death which sin brought into the world. But that sinlessness, as Karl Rahner goes on to point out was 'not an inheritance from the earthly Paradise (before sin spoilt it all) but the fruit of Christ's redemptive death on the Cross'.[9] Christ's pattern for redemption was death and resurrection, and Mary, who was the first fruit of that redemption, the most radical and complete, followed the pattern of her son with whose life her own was so entwined, and he died, really died, and then rose again.

Where and how Mary died we do not know. There are two traditions. One says she died at Jerusalem; if you go to the Holy Land, you will be shown the 'Tomb of Our Lady' at the foot of the Mount of Olives. The other tradition says that St John took Mary with him to Ephesus and that she died there. If you go to Ephesus they will show you the site of the house she lived in. I don't take sides in this discussion because I don't think that time and place are of any importance. It is the fact of her death that we are looking at now.

There are different ways of looking at death. One is to consider it as a punishment for sin, something destructive, contrary to nature, a traumatic experience that horrifies and revolts us, that we fight against though we must lose the battle. We die. Another viewpoint sees death simply as the end of our earthly journey and the entrance into eternity, a going home.

The leading up to it may be painful and extremely uncomfortable but the moment of death itself is swift and the happiness of Heaven is total and forever.

For each of us there is something of both these aspects in our own deaths. We are shop-soiled, seconds, sinners, so death frightens us, terrifies us even. But we are saved and death puts the final seal on our salvation. The case of Mary's death was different from ours, very different, she was sinless. Therefore the first aspect of death wouldn't have figured in her experience. The second would surely have been the way she met death. She had nothing to be afraid of. The greatest pain she suffered would surely have been that of separation from her son; that, death would put an end to.

We have seen that the pattern of redemption was death and resurrection. A pattern is something that repeats itself and so it is that, 'When we were baptised in Christ we were baptised in his death; in other words, when we were baptised we went into the tomb with him and joined him in death, so that as Christ was raised from the dead by the father's glory, we too might live a new life. If in union with Christ we have imitated his death, we shall also imitate him in his resurrection' (Romans 6:3–5).

So hope is held out to us! Yes, but it's awfully far away and misty. We find it hard to imagine ourselves coming to life again. It's all very well to tell us that life will be different, that we will each be the same person – this is true, but our bodies will be spiritual, glorified bodies. The truth is that no-one really knows what it will be like, and it is all so vague that we easily doubt.

Knowing all this, God bestowed yet another gift upon Mary, once more *for us*. Mary has already risen again. Scarcely had she died than God raised her up again and she was taken up ('assumed' is the word used) into Heaven. It was the short duration of her state of death that probably gave rise to the expression 'dormition', it was 'as if' she slept.

But how do we know that Mary was raised from the dead and was taken up into Heaven? It isn't in the Bible. I know it is not. I know that the Bible is the word of God and is absolutely true, but that does not mean that everything that is not in the Bible is untrue. We believe a lot of things in history without there being very much proof for some of them, and they certainly were not in the Bible. We are inclined to believe much of what we read in the papers, however conflicting the different accounts of the same events may be. We even believe advertisements however much some of them have us on. We do recognize that there are truthful people and they are worthy of our trust. Why then should we be so reticent when it comes to Christian tradition?

Certainly a great many weird and wonderful mythical tales were woven about the life and death of Mary during the first centuries of the Church and were further embroidered during the Middle Ages. In leaving these aside, as we should, we must also make allowance for the cultures of the times that expressed themselves differently from the way we do. But sorting through all the available sources we will find a strong, persistent tradition that Mary was taken up, body and soul, into Heaven very shortly after her death. It would be foolish to ignore this. I have not done this sorting and sifting myself, but I am willing to accept the uprightness and credibility of those scholars who have, and to take their word for it. Therefore I say that I do believe in the Assumption of Mary into Heaven. In so doing I share in 'the belief of the Church in the triumphant accomplishment of redemptive grace', and I 'confess what the Church defined: After the completion of her earthly life, Mary was assumed body and soul into the glory of Heaven'.[10]

We listen reverently and quietly to the recitation of Mary's other special gifts and are rather awe-filled while considering them, but when it comes to Mary's Assumption into Heaven (the Feast of 15 August) we are triumphant and exalting. At least people with strong faith are. That is why, in so many places, such a big fuss is made of the Feast of the Assumption. I remember well, when I lived in a mountain village in Lebanon, all the candles placed along the edges of the flat roofs of the houses (including our own), the village all ablaze with fireworks and noisy with bangers and the whole mountainside alight with bonfires – all to express belief in, and joy on account of, Mary's Assumption. It gave us all a great, up-lifting feeling that, although life might be rough at times, although we still had death to face and perhaps fear, our own resurrection would be waiting just round the corner. Mary had made it, and that was a pledge that we could too.

CHAPTER NINE

Nativity Play

Nouha came from one of the more remote mountain villages of Lebanon. There was none of the 'chocolate box' prettiness about her but she was a fine-looking girl with that dignity, integrity and self-possession characteristic of true peasants. Healthy and happy, she was well used to hard work and a very simply lifestyle. Though full of life and fun, there was just a touch of seriousness about her, due no doubt to the responsibility that fell upon her as being the eldest of a large family where resources had to be carefully measured and shared. (Her parents had wanted six boys and six girls, they got all the girls but the sixth boy never arrived.)

At school she was in the section for which I was responsible and would have been about fifteen or sixteen the year we did the Nativity Play. Nouha was chosen for the role of Mary. It was not the usual stable scene Nativity play traditional in Infants' school, but more symbolic. It had two acts. The first was the Annunciation, when the Angel Gabriel came to Mary to invite her to embrace the mission God had chosen her for.

The curtain opened as Mary came in carrying a jar of water on her shoulder. Gabriel came in at about the same time and addressed Mary who, surprised, put down her jar. The Angel then gave the message, using the words of Scripture. Mary did not answer immediately. Her mind was flooded by thoughts echoing the prophesies of the Messiah, the Suffering Servant. Also her heart went out to all the people, her own people, who were crying out to God to send them a Saviour. 'Shepherd of Israel listen, . . . rouse your strength, come to us and save us . . . let your face shine upon us and we shall be safe' (Psalm 80: (79) 1–3).

The audience was made aware of what Mary was thinking by two choirs, one of prophets and the other of people of God, who alternatively sang, in Psalm tone, and mimed, appropriately arranged verses of Scripture.

This took quite a long time (much longer than it would have taken Mary to think it) and during this time Mary stood in centre stage on a higher level than the choirs. She stood quite still, head erect, looking slightly upwards, deep in thought. Gabriel stood a little to one side respectfully awaiting her reply. Then she turned to him, inclined her head and said: 'I am the handmaid of the Lord,' and, with a wide gesture of receiving, folded her hands lightly on her breast. At that point a solo voice off stage sang quietly but distinctly, 'Et Verbum caro factum est.' ('And the Word was made flesh.') Gabriel genuflected and the two choirs kneeled and bowed low to the ground in adoration of the newly-conceived 'Word made man'. The curtain went down slowly upon this scene.

In rehearsing this act I realized that the role of Mary was particularly difficult to play. Anyone who has had anything to do with amateur dramatics, especially when children are involved, knows that there is nothing harder to do than to stand still on stage, totally inactive. Nouha had to do that, to do it for the whole scene and hold the centre stage all the time. She hadn't to move, much less fidget, and yet she hadn't to look stiff, awkward or self-conscious, and she had a tremendous message to convey.

To help her I took her aside and carefully explained the Annunciation story and the role she was playing. 'Nouha,' I said, 'If this is to be any good at all, if it is to ring true, you must forget everything else around you and enter right into Mary's thoughts and feelings. You've heard what the "People of God" are saying, how they are calling on Mary to say "Yes", because they need a Saviour so badly. Think of those people, think of them here in the hall. Among the audience there will be people of all sorts, with many kinds of problems and difficulties, family problems, health problems, financial problems, sorrows, pains, anger and more. There will be those in doubt, in darkness, those in temptation and those in sin. Think of them all and pray for them. Bring all of them, with all their troubles, to God and pray for them as hard as you can, all the time you are standing there and don't worry about how you look. Everything will be all right if you pray like that.' Nouha looked at me attentively and seriously, fixing me with her direct, clear gaze. 'Do you understand, Nouha?' I asked. She nodded and I went away humbled beyond measure at what I had asked that girl to do.

The big day came. I watched from the wings and was humbled even further by the simplicity, poise, earnestness and dignity with which Nouha filled her role. She never spoke to me about what passed within her during that time, and I, respecting her reserve, never questioned her. But after the play was over I was besieged by the audience whose whole admiration, astonished admiration, was for Nouha and the outstanding way she had portrayed Mary. And yet, she had done nothing, except just stand still!

No, she had done much more than that, she had portrayed Mary interceding, and intercession is an essential part of Mary's mission. I thought I had explained to Nouha Mary's role in our regard, but that day I learnt a lot more from that young peasant girl than I had taught her.

Yes, intercession is Mary's role. That is why we say so often: 'Holy Mary, Mother of God, pray for us – pray for us now, and at the hour of our death.' Mind you, we don't say: 'Holy Mary, pray for us,' but 'Holy Mary, *Mother of God* pray for us', because it is from that motherhood that stems not only her role of intercessor but also the power of her intercession. As just a human woman, just one of us, Mary's power of intercession would be no greater than anyone else's (not that I'm saying that our prayers for others are useless. Indeed they are not and we have a duty to pray for each other.) But, as Mother of God, Mary's intercession is another story. It is from the fact of her divine motherhood that her prayers for us, her own people, draw all their efficacy, a God-given efficacy and power which is infinite because the source is divine.

The Church speaks of the 'mediation' of Mary and calls her 'Mediatrix'. St Paul tells us that 'there is only one mediator between God and man, the man Christ Jesus' (1 Timothy 2:5–6). When we say that Mary is a mediatrix we are no way contradicting St Paul, or setting up Mary as an equal of, or rival to, her son. She is not a go-between either, getting between us and Jesus in a way that would block our relationship with him, of course not. But it was through Mary that Jesus came to us. She was the 'way' through which God chose to give us the Word, and, as a meteor draws a trail of stars in its wake, so Mary's intercession follows in the train of Jesus' mediation. Actually, if you do start by praying to Mary first, I don't think you'll do it for long, for the more you try to intensify your devotion to Mary, the more you will find yourself relating to Jesus, the more your devotion to him will grow. It's a way Mary has. She gives us Jesus and leads us to him.

This fact was brought out in the second act of the Nativity Play. The scene portrayed an altar ready for Mass. It was in pre-Vatican II days so there were the three big candles either side of the tabernacle. Angels held the candles and, in place of the tabernacle, was Mary (as much as any tabernacle she had contained him within herself when she conceived him in her womb).

At Mass the priest says: 'This is my body. This is the chalice of my blood,' and by these words Jesus is rendered present, born again so to speak, upon the altar. So Mary was holding the new-born Jesus in her arms. Mary was there, Jesus was there (he always is present when she is there) and all the people of God were there too. They were singing and praising, 'Glory to God on High', as the angels sang the first Christmas night, and telling of their joy at his birth and their desire to receive him into their lives.

'The body of Christ, the blood of Christ', says the priest in offering him in Holy Communion to the people. Mary smiled and, stretching out her arms, offered her child to all the people. She didn't speak, no words were necessary, the gesture was enough. He was her child, yes, but she didn't receive him for herself, much less to keep him from us, but to give him to us, to bring us nearer to him. Those who find Mary have indeed found their fortune for Mary always gives them Jesus.

Mary stands in a supportive, though subordinate role. She is always thinking of us and praying for us. If the people in that school hall were so impressed and in such admiration when a young peasant girl represented Mary, played her role for twenty minutes or so on stage, what should be our awe-filled and grateful attitude before, not the shadow, but Mary herself continually interceding for us?

CHAPTER TEN

A Leap in the Dark

If I let you see me put a handful of coins into my pocket, if I jingle them so that you can hear them, and then ask: 'Do you believe that I have money in my pocket?', perhaps you would answer: 'Yes, of course.' To which I would reply: 'No, you don't. You *know* by your senses, your sight and your hearing, that it is there.' That kind of knowing is not believing.

If I then tell you that, in another pocket, I have an expensive diamond ring and ask you to believe that I have it although you have no proof, you might hesitate and reflect. If you consider that I am an honest, truthful person whom you can trust, you will say: 'Yes, I do believe it.' That would be faith in my word.

This kind of faith, believing without proof, is not very popular nowadays. We want to be able to weigh, measure and examine everything and have the proof laid out before us. All the same, there must be a lot of blind faith about otherwise, for instance, advertising wouldn't pay. Just think of all the marvels we are asked to believe concerning the many products and offers advertised on our TV screens, in our papers and on bill boards. We are bombarded by this kind of thing all the time. Certainly many of us take much of this with a pinch of salt but all the same it is surprising how much we swallow. The advertisers know that, and so they know that advertising is very worthwhile. However when it comes to religious belief and creeds we are more inclined to doubt. (Though there are always crowds who will run after the latest cult, the more exotic the better!)

The faith I want to talk about isn't just an intellectual acceptance of a statement. No, it goes further than that. Take, for example, a parachutist. He or she doesn't simply believe that the parachute is reliable. The parachutist acts upon that belief. The parachutist jumps. The action confirms, proves, the belief. It's easy to say: 'Oh yes, I believe all right,' but when there's an occasion for putting that faith into action we feel, 'I'd rather not try it. You go first.'

Our faith does make demands upon us. Our principles of conduct are shaped and guided by what we believe and we are often under tremendous pressure to act otherwise. The stand we know we should take can be made to look so impractical and unreasonable, even stupid. Often we find it difficult to make certain decisions, to step out and follow certain lines of action. We look to see what other people are doing. We look for someone else to 'go first'.

If we want an example of someone who believed the impossible and accepted the unreasonable, someone who was just an ordinary person like ourselves and who was presented with an enormous decision to make, and one that would be very difficult to carry out, yet who made that decision and stood by it to the end, let us look at Mary. She 'jumped' first, and what an encouragement and help that is to us! 'You will bear a child without a father. He will be the Son of God. He will be the Suffering Servant of Yahweh with all that that implies for you. Will you do it?' That was the substance of the Angel's message to Mary. It sounded impossible, absolutely impossible. It sounded also as if it would involve a lot of pain. Mary said: 'Let all that happen to me'. 'Let what you have said be done to me' (Luke 1:38). Mary 'jumped' and it was a leap in the dark. Mary could do it because she believed. 'Blessed is she who believes' (Luke 1:45).

She believed because she 'heard'. She had heard the Angel, not just superficially but she received the message in her heart. The Angel told her in his own way: 'You won't have to do this alone. The Holy Spirit will do it in you. This is going to work. Your son will put everything right and his work will last for ever' (cf. Luke 1:26–38).

Mary knew the Scriptures, she was familiar with the promises of Yahweh and she took the Angel's word, she 'believed that the promise made her by the Lord would be fulfilled' (Luke 1:45). She didn't cross examine the Angel or look for evidence and proof. She heard and she believed.

Faith, St Paul tells us, comes through hearing. 'They will not believe in him unless they have heard of him, and they will not hear of him unless they get a preacher' (Romans 10:14). In other words, we have to take it on somebody's word. 'The righteous man will live by faith, but if he draws back, my soul will take no pleasure in him' (Hebrews 10:38 quoting Habakkuk 2:4).[11]

St Paul goes on: 'Not everyone, of course, listens to the Good News,' and he sums it all up with, 'so faith comes from what is preached, and what is preached comes from the word of Christ' (Romans 10:16–17). The word of Christ is the word of God.

On one occasion a woman in the crowd listening to Jesus was so thrilled with all he said that she cried out: 'Happy the womb that bore you and the breasts that you sucked' (Luke 11:27). She was right of course, Mary was happy to have been his mother, but it wasn't her physical maternity that was the most important thing. Something much deeper than that was the reason for her happiness – her relationship with God, which involved the hearing of God's word and acting upon it and which brought about her physical maternity. That is why Jesus replied to the woman in the crowd: 'Still happier are those who hear the word of God and keep it.' We too can share in Mary's happiness if we hear God's word and keep it.

Mary's faith was truly for us. It made her the mother of Jesus and so gave us a saviour. She was the one who 'went first' and gave us the lead. It is up to us to follow.

Looking at Jesus when he was a little lad just like any other little lad, Mary must have needed faith to believe that as well as being a little boy, her son was also really God. We know from the Gospels that there were times when she didn't understand but she believed. The Angel's message had meant that the ordinary woman, Mary, would become the extraordinary woman, the Mother of God. All the rest of her existence was not only coloured by that fact but transformed.

To us also an extraordinary transformation is proposed. From being ordinary human beings we can become children of God, sharing the divine life of Christ who comes to dwell in us. Do we believe in the indwelling of Christ in us? The ordinary way of receiving this divine son and daughtership is by baptism. (God, of course, can give it extra-sacramentally as well. God is never limited. We don't know anything about God's secret dealings with individual souls, we just know that baptism was instituted for that purpose.)

Baptism raises us from the ordinary level to an extraordinary one. This transformation was made possible by Mary's consent, in faith, to become Mother of God. God became man, Mary became the Mother of God and we became children of God. All as the result of Mary's faith.

CHAPTER ELEVEN

Making Friends

Have you ever had the experience of finally meeting a person of whom you have heard a great deal – not just in a formal, distant, passing manner, but in a way that brought that person right into your life? A relation who lived in a different country, Uncle Jo or Aunt Liz who went to live abroad when you were very young so that you didn't really know them, or perhaps your family moved so that you had never met your grandparents or cousins. So, you had heard one particular person talked about lots of times, you had even written letters to him or her. Perhaps you had been made to write and your letters were rather stiff, unreal and impersonal. Then one day you hear that this person is coming to live with you, in your house. You wonder what it will be like and are not very enthusiastic about it. Then, when you actually meet, you find in this stranger a real, live, warm, loving person and a great relationship builds up. All this is quite different from what you had expected because knowing *about* a person is quite a different matter from *knowing* that person.

This may be a little like our relationship with Mary. Do we know her, or only about her? What kind of relationship do we have with this most extraordinary woman who is also so ordinary, so warm, loving and so close to us? We know a lot about her without any doubt, but, still, do we know her?

There is only one way to get to know Mary, or to know her better if we have already met her, and that is to frequent her. We must often speak to her. I don't mean just recite prayers but to speak to her as we would speak to a real person, a friend who is very close to us and whom we love and trust, someone to whom we can say anything at all, no matter what kind of mood we may be in or how we are feeling.

Of course this is not quite the same as the way we meet our friends face to face. Our relationship with Mary, or with Jesus for that matter, is necessarily 'in the dark', in faith. As St Paul says: 'Now we are seeing a dim reflection ...' (1 Corinthians 13:12). Full vision will come later. So we need to put our imagination to work. One way is by meditation, imaginative meditation. That does not mean we are just making it all up, no, it's real but we are using our imaginations to visualize it.

We take one of the teachings in the Gospels, read it through slowly two or three times, then try to reconstruct the scene as clearly as possible in our minds. We note the details of form and colour and the positions of people and things, then, so to speak, we step into the scene identifying with someone there. It is important that we get into the picture and don't just play a kind of cinema film to ourselves. Forget everything else and just *be* there. This may take a little practice and some days it won't work at all, but it will come and will be very rewarding. Speak to the persons around you, especially Jesus and Mary and listen to what they say.

Before we go any further, just a word to allay some possible fears. Will not too much intimacy with Mary come between us and Jesus? In any case, is there any point in going to Mary? Why not just go straight to Jesus? Of course we can go straight to Jesus, and should do so, but having a chat with Mary in no way interferes with our talking to Jesus, especially as the biggest bit of advice we will get from Mary is to talk to Jesus more often!

Mary has only one interest and that is in her son Jesus. Her influence in our lives can do one thing alone, and that is draw us closer to Jesus. She will teach us to know and love him better. She will show us how we can best serve and please him. She will never, never take us away from him. But how will all this happen? Surely we can't expect visions or to hear Mary's voice telling us what to do. No, that's not the way at all. It somehow just comes about. When we are serious in our efforts to get to know Mary better we just find ourselves 'knowing' things or being more at ease with Jesus, or more interested. It is difficult to explain the precise 'how' but, as I said, it just comes about.

At Cana, Mary intervened when the bridal couple ran short of wine (which would have been a terrible disgrace), but see how she intervened. She sent the waiters to Jesus saying: 'Do whatever he tells you' (John 2:5).

Let's get back to our imaginative meditation and do something about it. Let's spend a quarter of an hour or twenty minutes stepping into that marriage feast at Cana and just being one of the guests. We may find that it is not only the water that is transformed but a transformation may begin to take place in us too. As we mix among the other guests we will make sure that we get near enough to Mary and Jesus to have a good view of what is going on. Note a certain uneasiness and whispering among the servers, and Mary's quick eye taking in the situation. Just imagine that you overhear Mary's remark to Jesus: 'They have no wine.' I can picture her little smile when Jesus seems to put her off: 'Woman why do you turn to me? My hour has not yet come.' Mary is tested like anyone of us but her smile seems to say: 'I know him better than that!' Anyway, quite unperturbed, she says to a waiter: 'Do whatever he tells you.' Jesus then tells the man to fill up the water jars. The waiter does so with the help of some of the other waiters and then stands wondering what is going to happen next. 'Draw some out,' says Jesus, 'and take it to the steward.' The man does so and, wonder of wonders, instead of ordinary water, the pots are full of beautiful rich wine!

In the meantime the young couple are totally unaware of what is going on. They are both on top of the world and think everything is just fine. And if it hadn't been for Mary's intervention they would have been very red-faced in front of the whole village.

Then I see Mary looking at me in a rather strange way, as if she had noticed something amiss in me. I don't feel exactly comfortable but she looks so kind that I get a little closer and whisper: 'Is there something wrong?' 'It's your shortcomings,' she answers, 'You have no wine.' She keeps on looking at me as if she could see right inside me. I know that it is not wine she is talking about but something else that I'm lacking. Perhaps it is kindness, or generosity, or truthfulness, or faith or something else. I think I know what it is and turn to her for help. 'Do whatever he tells you,' she whispers and moves aside so that I can get right beside Jesus and have a little talk with him. And, if I decide to do what I know he is telling me to do, what a difference it will make in my life. Perhaps not all at once but little by little.

Jesus is the great healer of all sinfulness and all brokenness and will change my stagnant water into clear, rich wine. Further, he will say: 'This is my body, this wine is my blood', and his divine life will flow more and more into me and make me live, not of my own life but of his life. All this because Mary said: 'You have no wine.'

Just reflect on that little exercise. Do you think that Mary came between Jesus and me, or has she not, rather, drawn me nearer to him? This is only one example of Mary's intervention in our lives. There are many other ways in which she takes an interest in us, helps us, strengthens us, encourages and consoles us, and always by bringing us closer to Jesus. But, like her son, Mary respects us and never tries to force our wills. She won't push herself into our lives if we don't want her. Only if we turn to her, speak to her, and listen for her answer in the quiet of our souls, will Mary come to our assistance; and when she does come, never will she let us down. She is waiting for us. Like Jesus she says: 'I am standing at the door knocking' (Revelation 3:20). If we will open to her and let her in and take the trouble to get to know her, we will be surprised and delighted with all she will do for us.

CHAPTER TWELVE

Turning the Handle

'I made that dress, didn't I, Mummy?'
'Yes, Darling, you were a great help.'

I was too young to go to school so I stayed at home with my mother. She used to make and mend all our clothes so she was often sewing. Her sewing machine worked manually and I used to want to turn the handle. If this was a help or hindrance, your guess is as good as mine! My guess is that I was dreadfully in the way. But my mother let me do it. She would tell me when to start, go fast, slow down or stop and she let me think that I was making dresses. I grew taller by the minute.

Of course, mothers reflect much of God's attitude in dealing with us, and so it is that God, who has no need of us at all, allows us, asks us even, to help in the great work of salvation and sanctification proper to Godself. And gave us Mary as a mother to show us how to do it and to guide us as we go.

We talk of 'evangelization' and busy ourselves in the 'Apostolate', and we tend to think that our contribution is essential and that we are converting and saving the world. We forget that God 'is not dependent on anything that human hands can do for him ... it is he who gives everything – including life and breath – to everyone' (Acts 17:25).

The Apostolate, however, is all-important and 'woe to me if I do not preach the Gospel (evangelize)' (1 Corinthians 9:16). But we must understand that the work is not ours, the means are not in our power and the results are certainly not due to us. It's all a case, as Mary taught us at Cana, of doing whatever Jesus tells us to do.

In other words, we must be completely available. Jesus is the great evangelizer and the Apostolate is his. Even so he was 'sent' by the Father and only did and said what the Father directed: 'The words I say to you I do not speak as from myself: it is the Father, living in me, who is doing this work' (John 14:10). We in turn must let Jesus live in us and act in us and through us. He then allows us to be his instruments and he rewards us as if it were we who had done it all: 'Well done my good servant' (Luke 19:17).

Mary understood this. 'Let what you have said be done to me,' she said, and as a result it was in her and through her that Jesus, the Saviour, came into the world and into our lives.

Mary was not the Redeemer, but because of her availability she gave us the Redeemer. Her role was so important in our salvation history that she is often referred to as the co-Redeemer. This does not mean that she was co-equally important in our redemption. No, her role was totally subordinate to his, but so closely linked that we give her this title. She was not our Saviour but she stood at the foot of the Cross, and his sufferings racked her very heart and soul. We might even say that our salvation was ratified as her motherhood of us was confirmed. 'This is your son. This is your mother' (John 19:26). For who is the kingdom for if not for Jesus' own brothers and sisters, those other children of Mary?

When Jesus said these words he was officiating as our High Priest, offering sacrifice for the sins of the people. 'He (Jesus) has done this once and for all by offering himself' (Hebrews 7:27). Without Jesus' sacrifice on the Cross there would have been no 'evangelization'. There would have been no 'Good News' to spread. We would not have been reconciled with God.

Jesus' sacrifice is perpetuated by the Christian priesthood, which is Jesus' own priesthood shared among us. The priest, ordained for that purpose, acts in Jesus' name when he offers the sacrifice of the Mass in obedience to Jesus' words, 'Do this as a memorial of me' (Luke 22:19).

Mary was not a priest. She was a lay woman, one of the laity like the majority of us – one of us. But if it is by the priesthood that the saving act of Christ is actualized, the laity have a very great part to play in the spreading of the Kingdom. I wonder if we always realize the extent of our responsibility? In people's minds the Church in the past was too often divided into the clergy and the laity; that is to say, the Shepherds and the Flock, the Teachers and the Taught. Very often that resulted in the Word being preached to the converted, as only they went to Church to hear it. But if the laity pull their weight in spreading the Good News in all kinds of situations, then the unconverted might also hear the Word of God!

We don't hear of Mary preaching the Word. Or do we? She did more than just preach, she carried the Word to the first Hearers of the Word, and that we may be sure she did on many, many more occasions than are actually mentioned in the Gospels. When the Angel left her after having brought her the Good News, we are told that 'Mary set out ... and went *as quickly as she could*' (Luke 1:39) to go to visit her cousin Elizabeth. Elizabeth was overjoyed, and at the sound of Mary's voice the child that Elizabeth was bearing 'Leapt for joy' (Luke 1:44). This was the very beginning of the spreading of the Good News, and we may be sure that Mary continued to spread it all her life and that very many people leapt for joy as a result.

She couldn't help taking Jesus to people, he was living within her. Not only when she was carrying him in her womb but all her life he lived in her as she, more than anyone else, lived by his life. So united was she to him, so infused was her soul with the divine life he had brought to share with humanity, that her life was entirely lost in his.

Too long we have had the tendency to think of Mary as the 'Madonna' of so many of our beautiful works of art. That's all right but I like to think of her more as a, quietly and very unobtrusively, very active lay woman, who, by the aptness of her words and gentleness of her manner, brought people to Jesus, and through him to the Father that Jesus was always talking about. She would have been extremely sensitive to people, as at the marriage feast at Cana, and would have gently but firmly guided people to her son.

On both of the two occasions I have mentioned, the time Mary went to visit Elizabeth and the wedding feast at Cana, Mary took the initiative. She set out to go to her cousin, and she spoke first, 'They have no wine.' And she didn't take an apparent 'No' for an answer. She had initiative and she was persevering. All the same it was Jesus' work not hers. The sound of Mary's greeting to Elizabeth would have had no effect on the child Elizabeth was carrying had Mary not been bearing the Saviour of the world. Mary worked no miracle at Cana but her advice to 'do whatever he tells you' had an effect.

So however important Mary's role might have been she was only 'turning the handle' for Jesus, who himself was doing his Father's work. That should put our own work of evangelization, our own Apostolate into perspective and by looking at Mary we will understand this better. Like Mary we don't convert the world alone, we don't work miracles to spread the Kingdom, but God wants us to participate actively, to take the initiative and to be persevering. This applies to lay men and women as well as to clergy, we all *have to* work for the Kingdom. That is what we were given 'talents' for, be it ten, five or one. We have no right to bury our talents but must put them to good use. In the Gospel story those who did so were commended but the servant who did nothing was sternly reproved (Matthew 25:16–30). But when all is said and done, the work is Christ's, not ours. Like Mary we are only 'turning the handle'.

CHAPTER THIRTEEN

The Twelve Months of Christmas

It was still weeks before Christmas and the shops were already being decked out with garlands. Father Christmas and snowmen, and fantasies of every kind, filled the windows. Fairy lights were being put up in the streets and a big Christmas tree stood at the entrance of the shopping precinct. It was all hollow, a tinsel festivity celebrating commercial enticement and financial profit.

But the choir leader was looking out the seasonal hymnals and had announced that, next week, the choir would start practising 'O Come Divine Messiah' and other Advent hymns and Christmas carols.

And nearly 2,000 years ago a teenage girl thrilled with expectation in the knowledge that this very Messiah, the Holy Anointed One, the Promised Saviour of the World would soon be born. He was coming, coming, oh so soon, yet she could hardly wait that last month of his coming. The waiting, the thousands of years of waiting of the Daughter of Zion, all seemed concentrated in those last few weeks, though the actual time of his coming was now so near. And that is what we commemorate and re-live during our four weeks of Advent.

'Advent' means 'coming' and in this, the first of the Church's 'seasons', we wait with Mary for the coming of the Word. Jesus came once when he was born at Bethlehem, but he still comes, for as well as coming once into the world historically, he comes personally into each one of our individual lives. He comes but there isn't always much room in our 'inn', so he comes again and again. Sometimes we reject him and push him out. Other times we open the door just a little, or perhaps a lot, but until every area of our lives has been opened out to him, he keeps on coming. Every year we think of this and try to remove some of the clutter that bars his way. 'Prepare the way for the Lord, make his paths straight' (Mark 1:3), cried John the Baptist.

So we turn to Mary who, herself, prepared so beautifully for his coming, carrying him herself those last nine months of his way. In union with her, we give ourselves up to joyful expectation, while trustfully repenting of anything we may be aware of in our lives that may be a blockage to his coming.

What we call the 'Liturgical Year' is just the Church's seasons following the principal stages of Jesus' life. 'Advent', the first of these seasons, fills the four weeks before Christmas. The person most concerned with an awaited birth is the expectant mother, so Advent is a time when Mary's presence is all-pervading, as we keep her company awaiting the coming of the Lord.

As soon as Christmas Day is over all the tinsel and decorations in the shops are pulled down and the sales begin. Now the shops sell off cheaply all that is left over after the Christmas shopping crescendo. It's a kind of anti-climax and leaves an empty feeling in the High Street. A whole lot of fever-filled expectation has been stirred up and now, with a flop, we are back to everyday, empty sameness.

But for the Christian there is Christmastide, when we celebrate the Birth of Christ and rejoice in his coming among us. The Cribs and the Christmas candles stay up and we have a great deal to ponder. This is a time for renewal. Nothing should be the same again and our hearts are full of joy as we sing our 'Gloria in excelcis'. Our lives are a continual 'beginning again' and Christmastide is the time for letting Jesus take over a little more of ourselves, asking him to be born in us so that we may really live more and more by his life. At this time of year we think of Jesus as the little Infant of the Crib. As a baby can't be separated from its mother (even if he be Godself!), we turn to

Mary and allow her to welcome him in our name. We ask her to help us to grow in understanding of the real meaning of this tremendous encounter between God and humanity, which is what Christmas is all about.

Traditionally, there are twelve days of Christmas which bring us to the Feast of the Epiphany on 6 January. But as Christ's coming is an on-going event in our lives, in one sense the whole Liturgical Year is Christmastide – twelve months of Christmas! Every time we go to Mass and the words of Consecration make Christ present once again in the appearance of the bread and wine, a little 'Christmas' takes place in our lives.

But the feast of the Epiphany is also there to be celebrated and a new season of the Church's year to usher in. 'Epiphany' means 'showing' or 'manifestation'. It commemorates the coming of the Three Kings, or Wise Men, from distant countries to visit the Infant Saviour and to worship him. This is a rather mysterious chapter of the Gospels (Matthew 2:1–12), perhaps because it is so prophetic. Jesus was not just a baby like any other, though he was just that too. He was the King and Centre of all creation and he had come for all humankind of every age and country and station. These mysterious personages, who came from afar to pay him homage, symbolize wonderfully all peoples of all times and places, no matter how 'far away' they seem to be. They came, and it was Mary who 'showed' her little child to them. The Lord of all was 'manifested' to all people by the intermediary of Mary, his Mother.

The 'ordinary time' after the Epiphany may be thought of as the 'growing up time' of Jesus. We're not told a great deal about this period, when Jesus grew from infancy to manhood, this 'hidden life' as it is often called. The Gospel says the he 'grew to maturity and was filled with wisdom and God's favour was with him' (Luke 2:40), and that 'Jesus increased in wisdom, in stature, and in favour with God and men' (Luke 2:52).

Growth takes time, and this time is very important though it isn't usually very spectacular. We don't *see* Christ growing in our lives. Nothing much seems to be happening. We don't seem

61

to be getting anywhere. Religion doesn't seem to be of much use. It's not what 'seems' that is important. When the eternal dawn breaks we will *see* and we will get a great surprise! In the meantime we must have patience and confidence. In a hidden way Christ *is* growing in our lives, unless we are deliberately refusing him space to grow.

Jesus' growth period took place at Nazareth where he was living with Mary and Joseph 'under their authority' (Luke 2:51). Just imagine it! Jesus, Godself, being under anyone's authority! He was Godself but he was also a real boy, and that human boy submitted to the authority of his parents. Would that we could live under the authority of Mary! We know where that would lead us. Do you remember? 'Do whatever he tells you to do.' Under Mary's tutelage we might grow a little quicker, in wisdom and in favour with God and with others.

When Jesus was grown up and sufficiently prepared to start his public life, he spent forty hard days in the desert under the guidance of the Spirit. We honour this period with the six weeks of Lent. Jesus fasted during this time and prayed. Lent is a time for us to make a little more effort to repent of anything in our lives that is not Christlike, to deepen our prayer life and to prepare ourselves to commemorate Christ's Passion and Death and to celebrate his glorious Resurrection.

'Lent' is usually interpreted as coming from an old Anglo-Saxon word, 'lencten' which means 'spring'. The Church's 'spring' season is not a gloomy time, even if it is penitential. It is a time of expectancy after the winter. The green blade will rise again and the harvest is promised: wheat for the mill and grapes for the press to give bread and wine, food for body and soul.

Mary's presence was very discreet during Jesus' public life. We don't hear much about her, but she couldn't have been very far away or she wouldn't have been at hand to come forward and stand at the foot of the cross on Calvary.

The sword predicted by Simeon (Luke 2:35) was turned in the wound and Mary, Christ's mother and ours, became the Mother of Sorrows. When we stop to think about it, we realize that the cause of her sorrow, the pain-filled death of her son, was brought about, not by Pilate or Herod or the Sanhedrin, but by our need to be reconciled to God. Much of that need is our own fault. By his sufferings he saved us, and Mary bore the brunt. The role she played in our salvation history is enormous. Can we ever forget it?

Pascaltide, or Eastertide, finds the Church exulting in the glorious Resurrection of Jesus. Zion rings to the cry of 'He is risen from the dead and he is Lord,' and the Church turns to Mary in her Easter prayer, 'Rejoice, O Queen of Heaven, for he whom thou didst merit to bear has risen as he said, Alleluia!' There it is, all in a nutshell. He couldn't have died and risen again if he hadn't been born, and for that he needed a mother. Now our salvation is assured and a pledge is given of our future resurrection and glorious eternity, and Mary has been near us all the time.

Mary was present again when the Holy Spirit, promised and sent by Christ, descended upon the Apostles as they were assembled with Mary in their midst. 'She who had been overshadowed by the Spirit and so conceived Jesus, now received the Spirit anew when the great wind blew, and the house shook and tongues of fire were visible resting upon the heads of all those present' (Acts 2:1–4).

We have a lot to think about as this season of Pentecost merges into 'ordinary time'. That is to say, a little marking-time space before we begin the whole cycle again. The leaves on the trees wither and fall, the snow covers the sleeping land and the green blade rises in spring again, as the seasons keep time with the Church's Liturgical Year. And the blue sky that we see from time to time reminds us of the discreet presence of Mary. There may be clouds at times but behind the clouds the sky is always blue.

CHAPTER FOURTEEN

Birthday Presents

Happy birthday to you,
  Happy birthday to you,
Happy birthday dear (Reader),
Happy birthday to you.

Yes, put your own name in and when the right date comes round I hope you have a very happy birthday. I hope also that you will receive some presents. If not, buy yourself one. That is what birthdays are all about.

As far as I know it is a universal custom to give people birthday presents. In any case it is a very apt custom as it can remind us that everything we have is a gift. In the first place we are in no way responsible for our own lives. Our life is something we receive. Then, when a baby is born its poverty is absolute. At birth, the child of the richest millionaire and the child of the most destitute of men have exactly the same – nothing at all. As Job said: 'Naked I came from my mother's womb' (Job 1:21).

As soon as a child is born, its parents, or other people, start giving it things. They have to or it will die. They give it clothes, nourishment, a cot of some kind. Then, according to the circumstances of the parents or guardians, other presents are added, from soft toys to bank accounts. Later the child is given an education, training and a means of eventually supplying for his or her own needs. Without being 'given' so much over so many years a child would never grow up able to provide for itself, so even his or her own earned livelihood and possessions are gifts. Inheritance also is a gift. Parents can disinherit a son or daughter. So nothing can be claimed as right of ownership. That is one of the things birthday presents can remind us of.

Birthday presents also tell us something else. They tell us of the love of those who give us presents. A present is a token of love. Those who make us a present are giving a little bit of themselves, and that bit is their love. A new born baby has done nothing at all to deserve that love. If just deserts were taken into account the baby mightn't be loved at all. Even before being born the little one may have cost the mother quite a lot of suffering. Some births have even cost the life of a mother. And most babies cost their parents a good deal of anxiety, loss of sleep, expense and very much more. So all the love that a baby receives is unconditional: not merited, not earned, just unconditional. Parents love their children, not for anything the child has done but because he or she is their child. After God they created it, and they are reflected in the child who is, in some way, an extension of themselves; the greater love they have for the child, the better the gift that is given to convey it.

The unconditional love received by a little child from its parents is just a feeble reflection of the immense, but totally unconditional love that God has for each one of us. God loves us because Godself created us and the image of the Godhead is reflected in each one of us. God points all this out when comparing this love to that of a mother, and goes further. 'Does a woman forget her baby at the breast, or fail to cherish the son of her womb? Yet even if these forget, I will never forget you' (Isaiah 49:15); and, 'Like a son comforted by his mother will I comfort you' (Isaiah 66:13).

That love God expresses in gift. First of all the whole act of creation is gift. But the fullness of God's gift is a share in God's own divine life which is not God but something of Godself, for God is love. Somehow we find it hard to believe in this tremendous, and totally unconditional, personal love of God for each one of us individually. Perhaps some of the hard knocks we have received in life may have contributed to this unbelief. Perhaps it is because we can't see or hear God that we think that the deity is impersonal. God knows that we have this difficulty so makes another gift to make it easier for us. God has given us Mary. She is one of us, a human being like us so we can easily relate to her, yet, she has always been so closely involved in the mystery of Christ, which is the mystery of God's love, that she is perfectly situated to help us make that leap of faith which is essential if we are to believe in God's love for us – a love which is expressed in Christ and in his Church. 'Mary will always be a key to the exact understanding of the mystery of Christ and of the Church'.[12] So Mary, especially the motherhood of Mary, will help us believe in God's love for us.

Why should Mary be considered to be such a big gift for us? Could we not, quite respectfully of course, leave her to one side? And, as she had fulfilled her purpose in bearing Jesus, could she not, so to speak, retire? Mary is one of us, a super one-of-us, perhaps, but one of us all the same and everything she received she received for us, in our name. Therefore she is essential to us. I think everyone must agree that she received the Word in her womb so as to give Jesus to us. In becoming mother of Jesus, mother of God, Mary received many graces, 'Hail full of grace,' the Angel said, (Luke 1:28). Some of these graces are often referred to as 'the privileges' of Mary. I don't like that use of the word 'privilege', it suggests special treatment to be enjoyed personally. None of Mary's 'privileges' were for herself alone. They were in view of, or as the result of, her motherhood of Jesus, and that was for us.

Mary was one of us, but we, the human race, were in a frightful mess. Corrupted at the source of our history, the river of human life flowed on polluted, and this pollution corrupts each human existence at its outset. This corruption, this pollution, is called 'sin', and 'The wage paid by sin is death' (Romans 6:23). Not a very cheerful or agreeable prospect!

We know that Jesus died to save us from all this ... but what assurance have we that it works? We want a demonstration, so to speak, of the effectiveness of redemption. Where do we get it? In Mary. Mary was redeemed, and what a glorious redemption that was! 'Although sinless, she was to represent, not the glory of the earthly paradise, but the perfect victory of the Grace of Christ in the weakness of the flesh'.[13] It was because her son died that she received this fullness of redemption as a tremendous birthday present. (In reality she didn't receive it at her birth but before that at the moment of her conception.) In this redemption we have our full share, it came to us through Mary's motherhood.

Looking at Mary we know that one of our own, in full solidarity with all our race, has made the grade perfectly. There are no loopholes we can latch onto and say: 'Yes, but perhaps ...' Mary stands out a shining light of hope for us, and each one of her 'birthday presents', the so-called 'privileges', rebound upon us giving us the joy and peace that come from the sure hope of our own redemption and eternal happiness.

So to find Mary is to find Jesus, and to find Jesus is eternal happiness. Have you found Mary? If you have you have found your fortune.

Crowning our Queen

Let's Pray It

There's a well-known story about a priest who was newly appointed to a parish. He went round visiting his parishioners and getting to know them. One dear old woman impressed him greatly; he felt that she was very near to God. This old lady was housebound and lived alone but she had a beautiful peaceful and contented expression.

'Well,' he said in the course of the conversation, 'at least you have plenty of time to pray. I expect you say very many rosaries.' 'No,' she smiled, 'I never say the rosary.'

Rather taken aback, the priest questioned her on the omission. 'I often begin to say the rosary,' she explained, 'but I never get past the Our Father; it's such a beautiful prayer that it takes me all day to say it.'

The priest was right in thinking that the woman was very near to God, and she was right in thinking that the Our Father, the prayer that Jesus taught us, was beautiful and rich enough to take all day over.

Now, if you can, really and truly, spend the whole day saying the Our Father, you have a very good reason for being excused from saying the rosary. Unfortunately, if you make that claim, I'm not at all sure that I won't take it with a pinch of salt. I know I could not pray like that even if I had the time! So I think we'd best get out our beads and say the rosary!

A lot of people nowadays seem to have gone off the rosary. I don't know if it's because they consider it to be boring, or old fashioned or monotonous or what. That's all nonsense, of course, the momentous events in the lives of Jesus and Mary are not subject to fashion and anyone who thinks them boring just hasn't a clue. After all, pondering these events in our minds is what the rosary is all about. But of course there can be abuses as the following example will show.

'Oh Sister,' a lady once wailed to me over the 'phone, after coming back from a parish pilgrimage to a shrine of Our Lady, 'Sister, it was awful, we said eight rosaries in the coach!'

Of course that was awful. That kind of thing is enough to put anyone off saying the rosary. In any case, when people say the rosary like that they usually don't *pray* it, if anything they *bray* it. That won't do at all and really is awful.

If you are going to say the rosary in common, perhaps it is best to say it with a few like-minded people, and say it quietly and unhurriedly, otherwise say it by yourself. Some people like to say it in their minds, others prefer to say it quietly under their breath. You can please yourself over this, the important thing is to *pray* it.

I said just now to take out our beads. Our rosary beads are important. They not only help us not to lose our place, but they also remind us of what we are doing when we get distracted. Besides, if you are a fidgety person your beads keep your fingers busy and so help you to remain peaceful. A rosary you like, one you are familiar with and which perhaps has rich associations for you, is more helpful than just any set of beads to which you are indifferent. You can have quite a relationship with your rosary and that has the psychological effect of helping you to like saying the rosary.

Finally, Mary seems to like us saying the rosary. She has said as much at many of her different apparitions. It's a beautiful prayer, summing up as it does all the more important joys of Mary, as well as all the events which caused her most pain, followed by the glorious, triumphant outcome of her life, so hope-giving to us who are sometimes rather overpowered by sorrow. Besides, all these thoughts are like melodies which for accompaniment have the words we say, which are Jesus' own prayer, the Our Father and the prayer the Angel Gabriel brought from heaven, the Hail Mary which Mary's cousin

Elizabeth added a bit to, and which the Church finished. Then we also have the Glory be to the Father which is the purest of all praise because we just don't think of ourselves in it at all.

If you are one of those people who have always loved saying the rosary, perhaps the following pages will help you to love it even more. If, on the contrary, you are turned off the rosary, hopefully they may help to turn you on again. If this latter is the case it might be a good idea to start by saying just one decade but say it rather slowly and thoughtfully, and then gradually go on to saying two or more decades until you are quite happy saying the whole rosary. Just reflect quietly on the mystery, turning over the ideas presented here in your mind, and asking the Holy Spirit and Mary (they work very well together) to make them come alive in you. You may not want to stick to these ideas and may have thoughts of your own about the mysteries – if so, so much the better!

It is customary to say the joyful mysteries on Mondays and Thursdays, the sorrowful mysteries on Tuesdays and Fridays, and the glorious mysteries on Wednesdays, Saturdays and Sundays. There is no obligation to keep to this arrangement, it just assures that you reflect on all the mysteries in turn. Of course, you may have your favourite mysteries, or make up others of your own, drawn from scenes from the Gospels. For example you could have the 'Jesus and sinners' mysteries, or 'Jesus and women' mysteries. A favourite of mine is the one described earlier, the wedding feast at Cana, so you see you can be very free in all this. The rosary can't be boring if you do all this. The boring thing would be to just rattle your beads and mumble or bray the Hail Marys.

The Joyful Mysteries

CHAPTER SIXTEEN

The Annunciation

'Hi Carol!'
      'Hi Jack!'
'Listen, my beautiful, I have some stunning news for you.'

That conversation sounds quite normal. That's the way people talk nowadays. Of course, long ago and in other countries the language people used was different. When the Angel Gabriel was sent to Mary their conversation was very different from the one above, but it wasn't the rather artificial scenario we sometimes picture it as being. So it was that Gabriel didn't say 'Hi' or 'Hello' to Mary but 'Hail'. It was quite a natural thing to say and meant 'Peace be with you'. (I don't know what 'Hi' means, just 'Hi' I suppose.)

The Angel certainly had some stunning news for Mary, and she was very taken aback. I would be taken aback if I saw an angel, wouldn't you? As for the message, well, it was the most stunning news that has ever been given at any time, anywhere in the whole world.

First of all the Angel addressed Mary as 'full of grace'. It's hard to understand exactly what grace is because it is something that relates to God, and we just can't understand God. But the Angel said that Mary was full of it, and we can guess that there was nothing more beautiful. Anything we have (and Mary was one of us) comes from God and in some way reflects God in us, as a mirror will reflect the sun. Of course, a tarnished or cracked mirror won't reflect much. Mary was *full of grace* so she was neither tarnished nor cracked, so she must have fully reflected the light of God. She must have been a perfect mirror.

In fact Mary was perfect. She always had been, even before

she was born, from the very moment of her conception. That is what the Church means when she talks about the 'Immaculate Conception'. It was God's way of preparing Mary for the wonderful role she was to fill and which was the subject of the stunning news she was going to hear.

God was going to come right into our humanity and have a human nature like ours. That meant that God would become a baby like any other baby, and would grow up to manhood as our Saviour. Actually this was going to be a two-way trans-action: God would share our human nature and enable us to share in the divine nature of God, without which we wouldn't be capable of enjoying eternity with God, that is, we wouldn't be able to go to Heaven.

Now, this baby needed a mother, and the message Gabriel brought to Mary was nothing else than an invitation to become that mother. What exactly that message conveyed to Mary we can only surmise. She knew the Scriptures, she knew that a Messiah, a Saviour, was to come. She knew the passages about the Suffering Servant. She knew all this was momentous even if she didn't immediately grasp how it fitted in with the message the Angel brought her. But for Mary there was only one possible answer, 'Yes'. She queried the 'How' of her motherhood as she was a virgin, but the Angel assured her that the Holy Spirit would be entirely responsible for her pregnancy. Then she had no hesitation, her answer was simple: 'I am the handmaid of the Lord' (Luke 1:38).

The word 'handmaid' in Mary's reply is very important. Actually the Aramaic word she would have used meant more a 'slave' than a simple servant. A slave is one who entirely belongs to another, who therefore fully carries out the will of that other. Nowadays we know that slavery is out, no-one can possess another person like that. We don't even want to be servants, but, whether we believe it or not, whether we want it or not, we do belong to God. We often resist God's authority over us and want to be on top, even with God! Mary had more sense than that. She understood what we find so hard to grasp, that is to say, the extent of our nothingness apart from God, and our total dependence on God.

God can, and is willing, no, anxious to fill that empty nothingness of ours with grace, and make of us something big and beautiful, but that can only be in proportion to how far we let God do this. Mary was empty of herself so she was full of grace, full of God. Mary said 'Yes' to God: 'Let what you have said be done to me' (Luke 1:38), was what she said. She put up no obstacles, no barriers or limits, so God filled her completely. She became pregnant with God.

The Angel went away, but in those few minutes something tremendous had happened. God had taken on human nature. God had entered humanity and become one of us, and Mary had become a mother, Mother of God.

With Gabriel and all the angels in heaven let us say: 'Hail Mary, full of grace ...'

CHAPTER SEVENTEEN

The Visitation

Travel agents are booming just now. If you go to an airport, railway or bus station, or just travel by car along the motorway you can't help but notice the number of people who are on the move.

In Mary's day there were neither aeroplanes, trains nor cars, the only way of getting about was on a donkey, or perhaps a camel, or on foot. The roads were bad, just tracks really, and there was always danger from thugs and brigands. Under these conditions people travelled only when it was really necessary.

Mary obviously considered her journey to be necessary. We are not told of her reasons for going to see Elizabeth, only that her cousin was pregnant, miraculously so, as she was elderly and past the age of child-bearing.

It would hardly have been likely that a young girl like Mary would travel alone. Did she ride? Did she walk? We don't know. Possibly she joined a caravan going the same way: Like this she would arrive at Elizabeth's home 'in the hill country of Judah' (Luke 1:39). Tradition points to Ain Karim, not far from Jerusalem.

The meeting between Mary and Elizabeth was very important. Mary was carrying a tremendous secret. She was pregnant with God, and no-one else knew! Yet when she met Elizabeth, her cousin greeted her as 'the mother of my Lord' (Luke 1:43). 'Lord' was a title of divinity, so Elizabeth knew too! We don't know how she had come to know this but as only God and Mary knew, and Mary hadn't told her, it must have been God who, in some mysterious way, had revealed the secret to Elizabeth. God has ways of communicating that are not ours.

Elizabeth knew, that is all we are told. Perhaps Mary learnt from this that Godself would make the secret known to those who should know it. Perhaps that is why, later on, she didn't tell Joseph, but let him suspect her until God stepped in and told him in a dream that Mary was all holy.

Mary responded to Elizabeth's greeting with the beautiful hymm of praise that we call the 'Magnificat' (Luke 1:46–56). In extolling God's greatness she again insists on her own lowliness, and says that the wonderful thing that has happened to her is all God's doing. She tells us, in no uncertain terms, that we won't get anywhere by being proud, or powerful, or rich, or big and important in any way. All that kind of thing only blocks God's action in us.

God wants a free hand to do great things in us and with us, and all our self-puffing-up gets in the way. No wonder God throws it all down. With Mary, God had a free hand with the result that through her, because of her son, we can all be lifted up to true greatness and eternal happiness and glory. The first person to receive grace through Mary was Elizabeth's son, John the Baptist. He wasn't even born at the time but Elizabeth tells us that 'the moment your greeting reached my ears, the child in my womb leapt for joy' (Luke 1:44).

We also would leap for joy if we would listen to Mary, and we would rejoice with her because of all the wonderful things that God has done for her and does for us. With all the generations we will call her blessed, and in blessing Mary we are really blessing God whose love and mercy all her holiness and happiness were due.

Let us join in with all those many generations of men and women who have called Mary blessed and say: 'Hail Mary, full of grace ...'

CHAPTER EIGHTEEN

The Nativity

If you give a really poor person £5 or £10 he or she will be grateful, but if you were to offer that sort of money to a business tycoon or a pop star they would be insulted. Mind you, they wouldn't be insulted if you offered a quarter of a million, except that they might say that wasn't enough. How great their need must be if all that money is required to fill it. How poor they must be! They may think that they are rich, but only a really, really rich person is rich enough to need nothing. God is that person.

God owns the whole world and everything in it. God doesn't need anything we can provide. Perhaps it was to bring that home to us that God chose to be born as a human being without any of the trappings of human wealth.

Then there is also another point. It is true that Jesus is God, and as God, owns the world, but Jesus is also a real man and in his humanity he, like Mary and the rest of us, is a creature, and as such is nothing. His divinity could only inhabit a human nature that recognized its native nothingness, and didn't try to usurp anything of the Godhead. So it could also be to highlight that human nothingness, that Jesus was born in, well, destitution. As St Paul says: 'His state was divine yet he did not cling to his equality with God but emptied himself to assume the condition of a slave and became as men are' (Philippians 2:6–7).

You can sentimentalize for ever over the sweet little Baby Jesus in the crib at Christmas, but if you do, you are missing the whole point. He may well have been a sweet little baby, most babies are sweet, but the mystery that was enacted that first Christmas was that God, who had taken human nature in the womb of Mary nine months earlier, was born into the world. The great Creator, and the nothingness that is a creature, were united for ever in the person of that little child, Jesus born of Mary. Born into the world for the express purpose of reconciling the human race, the straying human race, to God once again. He came as a saviour so that we also could be united to God and have a share in the divine nature, not only during this life, but for all eternity. No wonder that at the crib we should not only prostrate ourselves in adoration but also pour out our hearts in gratitude and love!

Of all those who saw the infant Jesus at Bethlehem, the only person who was able to really grasp anything of all this was Mary, and she 'treasured all these things and pondered them in her heart' (Luke 2:19). Mary must have had a most wonderful simplicity and loving trust in God to have been able to recognize how small and weak she was, and at the same time to know that she was really and truly mother of God! She must have had great faith to believe that her little baby, so small and weak as he was, was Godself. Surely it was only because she so well understood that littleness is the condition of God's being able to take hold of a person and do great things in him or her, that she was able to accept that her tiny child was her son and also her God. Certainly it was in her lowliness that her greatness lay.

Let us ask Mary to obtain for us the grace to recognize and adore God in Jesus, and to recognize Jesus in all the little ones of this world. And let us say with all our hearts: 'Hail Mary, full of grace ...'

CHAPTER NINETEEN

The Presentation in the Temple

It is easy to dismiss old people: 'A bit geriatric, you know, the poor old dear.' Perhaps the clever people of the time may have thought that anyone would have to be a bit geriatric to haunt the Temple continually as Simeon and Anna did, as if there was nothing more in life than that.

Simeon and Anna may have been very old but they certainly were not geriatric. In fact they knew a thing or two that Godself had told them. No-one else would have been able to tell them as no-one else knew. They knew, for example, when they saw a poor couple coming in carrying a baby, that that child was the Saviour of us all.

The old man had been looking out for the Messiah for a long time as, 'it had been revealed to him by the Holy Spirit that he would not see death until he had set eyes on the Christ of the Lord' (Luke 2:26). Anna also recognized the Christ and, 'began to praise God; and she spoke of the child to all who looked forward to the deliverance of Jerusalem (Luke 2:38).

This is the event we are gazing at in this fourth joyful mystery of the rosary and, the highlight of the day, was this recognition of God in a tiny child, by a holy old man and a saintly old woman.

Mary and Joseph had brought the child into the Temple to comply with the law. That in itself is a lesson for us, that laws aren't just to be brushed aside. It often takes a lot of faith to accept that there is something of God's authority in all lawful legislation and that by complying we are obeying God.

81

Simeon and Anna respected the law certainly, but that was because they lived in the presence of God and were people of prayer. They communicated with God and so it is not surprising that God communicated with them.

Now they had actually seen and touched the expected Messiah. They had not made the mistake of looking for someone great and powerful. Greatness and power belong to God, but the Messiah was a man as well as God, and it was fitting that the man part of him should be very small. Simeon took him into his arms and thrilled! He had nothing more to live for and looked forward with joy and peace to the time he would leave this world for a better one: 'Now, Master, you can let your servant go in peace' (Luke 2:29), he said, all his longings fulfilled.

But Simeon had a word for Mary too, a prophecy concerning the child and herself. All wouldn't be plain sailing. The coming of the Messiah would present a challenge that not all would accept. That would be a terrible responsibility and would be the downfall of some. As for Mary, she was to learn that being the mother of the Saviour would involve her in suffering: 'A sword will pierce your own soul too' (Luke 2:35), was the message Simeon had for Mary. Her son was the Suffering Servant of Yahweh, and her life would be inextricably entwined with his. He would save us by the Cross and she would become the Mother of Sorrows.

Let us thank Mary for accepting to identify with the saving sufferings of her son, and ask her to help us to be brave in carrying our own crosses in the footsteps of Jesus so that, like the drop of water in the wine at Mass, they may be transformed. Thus they will be part of the saving cross of Christ who, in us, will really be carrying our crosses. Let us bow our heads at the thought of our little generosity and courage and turn to Mary as we say: 'Hail Mary, full of grace ...'

CHAPTER TWENTY

The Finding in the Temple

That a teenager should go missing is unfortunately no uncommon occurrence nowadays. The anguish that the child's parents must go through is heart-rending.

I just wonder if Mary had to go through this experience, in her case so seemingly unnecessary, so that she might be able to empathize to the full with the, all too many, mothers throughout the centuries who, one way or another, have suffered the loss of a child?

We must remember that Jesus was not just a child, an individual child, though he was that. In taking human nature, the Son of God assumed all humanity. He identified with each one of us, and so Mary is the mother of every one of us individually. As such she is solicitous for the safety, especially the spiritual safety, of each and everyone, of you and of me. If at any time we are, even temporally 'lost', the pain of that loss was suffered in her loss of the Child Jesus (as, mercifully, she can't suffer now).

I discussed the loss of Jesus in the Temple at some length in my book *Prophets of Joy*. Here, it will be enough to say that the Holy Spirit was guiding Jesus and directing his life. As for Jesus, the boy, he was a normal boy and, as a child he made a child's judgement, when he stayed behind in Jerusalem. He expected his human parents to know that he would be doing his 'Father's business' and, totally engrossed in the doing of it as he was, it wouldn't have occurred to him that they would worry.

What teenager does not seek to establish his or her identity? Jesus was doing just that. Growing out of babyhood and early childhood, he was realizing more and more who he was and, coming to the age of religious adulthood in a Jewish boy's life, he went to the religious leaders in the Temple – his Father's house – to confirm the growing knowledge he had of himself.

The outcome of the whole incident was a happy one. Led, no doubt by the Spirit, Mary and Joseph found Jesus in the Temple, after he had been missing for three days. Their delight is understandable and is the object of this fifth joyful mystery.

Mary knew that her son was to be the Suffering Servant of Yahweh, so perhaps on this occasion she thought that that was it, he was already being taken from her to begin his difficult mission. She had learnt that as mother of the Messiah she would have suffering to bear, a sword would pierce her soul. The sword must have been hurting terribly during those three days of separation and uncertainty, therefore so much the greater was her relief and joy when Jesus was returned to her, safe and sound.

If I have compared the sorrow of Mary at the loss of Jesus to her sorrow at the spiritual loss of one of us, I can also compare the joy of Mary on finding her son, to her joy experienced in Heaven, when one of us sinners is found again. Holy Mother of God, pray for us sinners now, and at the hour of our death!

Pray for us she surely does continually. That is her role of intercession in Heaven, and rejoice she certainly does too, when we arrive safe and sound at the heavenly gates when our day is done. 'Rejoice with me, I have found my sheep that was lost.' 'In the same way, I tell you, there will be more rejoicing in Heaven over one repentant sinner than over ninety-nine virtuous men who have no need of repentance' (Luke 15:6–7).

Mary rejoiced when Jesus was restored to her and went back with her to Nazareth, where he lived in obedience to her and to Joseph. Let us also give her cause to rejoice in our obedience to God's will as we say to her: 'Hail Mary, full of grace ...'

The Sorrowful Mysteries

CHAPTER TWENTY-ONE

The Agony in the Garden

I have often wondered where Mary was those last few days of Jesus' life. She must have been in Jerusalem because she was present at the crucifixion. In those days, when there were no modern methods of transport or communication, she couldn't have travelled from any considerable distance in just a couple of hours or so. She certainly wouldn't have been in the garden that night when Jesus was arrested. Possibly when the disciples all ran away one of them went and told her what had happened, but she would have had to have been near at hand for that.

Even a very ordinary mother knows when her child is in trouble. It's something to do with maternal instinct and the bond there is between mother and child. Mary was more than just an ordinary mother. Her sinlessness must have made her extra sensitive, and because of the very special nature of their relationship, the bond between Mary and Jesus must have been very strong. So Mary *knew* that Jesus' hour had come. She certainly didn't sleep that night. The very fact that she didn't know *what* was happening, though she knew well enough that it was happening, must have made it worse.

Jesus, as man, was struggling with God. Shrinking, as he naturally was, from the terrible ordeal that awaited him, he cried out: 'Father, everything is possible to you. Take this cup away from me' (Mark 14:36). He didn't want to suffer and die. He wouldn't have been truly one of us if he had wanted it or if he had been indifferent. But his love of God and obedience to the divine will for our salvation prevailed and enabled him to overcome his natural human dread and resistance, and he added: 'But let it be as you, not I, would have it.'

Much has been surmised and written about what really constituted the agony of Jesus in the garden. We don't know, but the intensity of his sufferings is demonstrated by his sweat of blood. Extreme fear, pain and anguish do cause people to sweat, but not blood. It must have been more than the fear of physical pain and death that caused that sweat.

Jesus was there in the stead of all humanity. He had assumed humanity so the whole human race was incorporated in his person. When we think of all the sin and crime and malice and wickedness of all kinds that have been committed through the ages in every part of the world (including or own contribution), we can find no word strong enough to express the guilt that lay upon the manhood of Jesus that night. Perhaps the horror of it all was what caused his sweat of blood. He accepted the guilt and the expiation of it, for the Father's will it was that, by this expiation, the human race should be redeemed and relieved of a burden it could not carry itself.

Mary also, must have been enduring her own struggle. Like Jesus, she had known for some time that he was a target for murder. So, like Jesus, she also set out for Jerusalem where the crime was to be committed. Like Jesus she didn't want the suffering, either for her son or for herself, and like Jesus, she said: 'Let what you have said be done to me.' Like Jesus, too, she would have put herself in God's hands, and like him she would have received strength.

This, I know, is all surmising, but the evidence all points to it. The next day, Friday, she 'stood at the foot of the Cross' (John 19:25). She didn't faint or get hysterical, she stood. It could only have been that she had had her agony and had come in total trust, to total acceptance of God's plan for us.

The hour for Simeon's prophecy to be fulfilled had truly come this time. The sword of sorrow went right through her heart, and if it bled, the drops of blood mingled with Jesus' sweat of blood as he lay on the hard, bare rock in the garden.

Let us tremble and repent as we say: 'Hail Mary, full of grace ...'

CHAPTER TWENTY-TWO

The Scourging at the Pillar

News travels very quickly on the grapevine, so I don't doubt that Mary was kept well informed as to all that happened that Thursday night and Friday morning. She can't have failed to hear how Jesus was brutally lashed until he was one great wound.

It's all very well to read about this, it is quite another thing to be part of the picture. Policemen and firemen often have to witness terrible things, as when they have to cut a mangled body out of a smash-up on the motorway. Yet this was different. It was different because it was carried out deliberately with premeditation and hatred and with triumphant gleefulness. The difference was even greater as the victim was no other than the Holy One of God.

Isaiah had seen it all prophetically: 'I made no resistance, neither did I turn away. I offered my back to those who struck me . . . And yet ours were the sufferings he bore, ours the sorrow he carried . . . Yet he was pierced through for our faults, crushed for our sins. On him lies a punishment that brings us peace. (Isaiah 50:5–6 and 53:4–5).

Mary most surely knew the Scriptures. She would have been very familiar with these verses from Isaiah. Doubtless she had often pondered them, perhaps without fully understanding their meaning. Now she knew all too well. Although, mercifully, she wasn't present at the terrible scourging of her son, surely, with Isaiah's words ringing in her ears and her mother's sensitivity, she was more clear-sighted than any prophet and saw it all with her inward vision and felt the laceration as if she herself were suffering it.

This scourging was the first of the physical sufferings inflicted upon Jesus during his Passion. He had suffered mentally during his agony in the garden, he had been the object of hatred, he had been despised, scorned as a fool and taunted, now it was physical. The whole man had to suffer, and as Isaiah made quite clear, it was in the stead of the whole of humanity. That Jesus was treated with violence reflects the violence which human beings have inflicted upon one another in so many places throughout the ages.

What Jesus suffered in his own person was totally unjust, wickedly unjust, but what he suffered standing in the stead of all humanity was merited. It was not merited by Jesus himself, but it was merited by humanity as a whole, and here Jesus was taking the place of humanity. In becoming a man the Son of God became all men and women, he became humankind, and humankind had rashly and boldly turned aside from God, not following the path that leads to happiness and Heaven. All other paths lead to darkness and destruction. God did not will that. God wanted humankind to be eternally happy. So the Son of God became identified with humankind so that humankind could become identified with Christ and thus gain entrance into Life.

When we have pain or sorrow to bear and complain or revolt against it, let us remember the sufferings Jesus bore for us, and with humility and repentance let us turn to Mary and say: 'Hail Mary, full of grace ...'

CHAPTER TWENTY-THREE

The Crowning with Thorns

Mary would have hurried to Pilate's residence when she heard that Jesus was there, being tried. She must have done, otherwise, with all the crowd there was about in those narrow streets, she wouldn't have been able to follow him to Calvary, where we know she was at the crucifixion.

Standing outside Pilate's house she would have been able to catch a glimpse of Jesus when Pilate had him led out and shown to the people: 'Here is the man,' Pilate said, and Mary looked at her son wearing the iniquitous crown of thorns, while all the people shouted: 'Crucify him' (John 19:5–6).

A crown of thorns on his head! Surely there is a wealth of meaning behind this terrible scene. Physically it was a cruel torture. The thorns weren't the little prickles you find on garden roses, and they can be painful enough. No, the plant that would have been used has great thorns two or three inches long, and the soldiers would not have been gentle when 'they hit Jesus about the head' (Matthew 27:30). But deeper than this is a mystery that underlies the whole story.

Jesus' personality extended over a far vaster sphere than that of any other person. It is true he was what he appeared to be, a real man located in time and place. He was also, as we have already seen, more than that as he had taken all humanity to himself. He stood there as humankind, humankind in one person. Jesus is the head and we are the members of one body, the 'Mystical Body of Christ' (at least, we are the potential members, as we can fall out). But Jesus has the specific role of Head. 'If we live by the truth and in love, we shall grow in all ways into Christ, who is the head ...' (Ephesians 4:15).

This cruel act of crowning Jesus with thorns strikes directly at his Headship. If the powers of Evil could have decapitated Jesus the implication would have been devastating. It would have suggested that humankind had been separated from its head. As it is the Head was crowned.

The crowning was performed in cruel mockery, but the mockery was not able to take away the symbolic meaning behind the act of crowning. Crowning is for kings. In spite of themselves, the powers of Evil were, by this very act, proclaiming the kingship of Christ.

Kingship hasn't the 'punch' nowadays that it had in days gone by. This crowning of Christ took place at an epoch when kings were held in high honour and esteem. Further, for the Jewish people of the time, kingship would have evoked the memory of the great King David and the Jewish Kingdom. The king, for the Jews, held a sacred role, he was appointed by God: 'Yahweh has searched out a man for himself, after his own heart and designated him as leader of the people' (1 Samuel 13:14). More than that, the king received sonship of God: 'I will make his royal throne secure forever. I will be a father to him and he a son to me' (2 Samuel 7:14). And: 'He will invoke me, "My Father, My God and rock of safety", and I shall make him my first born, the Most High for kings on Earth' (Psalm (88)89:26–27).

David was a figure of the Messiah to come, now Jesus fulfilled that prophecy. He, the Son of God was King, as he had declared to Pilate, adding, 'Mine is not a kingdom of this world (John 18:36).

The Head was crowned, the kingdom was at hand. Speaking of his Crucifixion Jesus had said: 'When I am lifted up from the earth I will draw all men to myself' (John 12:32). Thus the unity of the body would be confirmed. This oneness should make us realize that the crowning with thorns was not for Jesus alone, but for the whole body. What the head enjoys, or suffers, is shared by the whole body. Jesus was crowned with thorns.

Sometimes these long thorns reach us and we feel their piercing, perhaps cruelly. When this happens let's turn to Mary, who feels with us as she felt with her son, because we are one with him, her children, and let us say: 'Hail Mary, full of grace ...'

CHAPTER TWENTY-FOUR

The Carrying of the Cross

Jesus often said mysterious things. At one time he said: 'Anyone who does not take his cross and follow in my footsteps is not worthy of me' (Matthew 10:38). What could the disciples have made of that? After all, they didn't understand that Jesus was going to carry a cross and be crucified. We have hindsight. We know what happened, but do we understand it?

Before the actual crucifixion took place, Jesus had to drag a heavy cross through the rough, bumpy roads of Jerusalem, and up the hill of Calvary. Whether it was the whole cross or just the cross beam, as some commentators think, is of no importance. The cross beam alone would have been very heavy, and Jesus was in no state to carry anything. And the shame and disgrace of carrying the instrument of criminal punishment was the same. The journey must have been a nightmare.

According to tradition quite a lot of things would have happened on the way. Jesus would have come face to face with his mother and then been pushed roughly on. Mary certainly would have been somewhere near, and what she felt is beyond our imagining. She would have been witness to his stumbling and falling, to his being kicked and whipped to get up, and his falling again. She would have been grateful to Simon of Cyrene for taking some of the weight of the cross off her son, and loved Veronica for wiping his face and the group of women for showing their sympathy. Jesus' words to the women would have reached his mother and she would have shuddered at his prophecy of the catastrophe that was to come.

We go to church and make the stations. In doing so, we might be tempted to think that we are following Jesus carrying his cross. That would be too easy and would certainly be missing the point. To follow Jesus we must first take up *our own* cross, as Jesus had said. When we do have a cross to carry we often think that we are hard done by, that it isn't just. We are full of self-pity and anger. This is not being logical. The Head carried his cross, and the disciples – the members of Christ's Mystical Body – must carry theirs after him. Rather it is one and the same cross: Christ's cross and our cross are one.

We are individuals and our crosses belong to us as individuals, it is true, but that is only one side of it. Our oneness with Christ is the other side, and that makes our crosses, so to speak, extensions of his cross. So we are just other Simons, helping Jesus to carry what is really his cross. We often do this unwillingly, as no doubt, Simon did to start with. But if we are generous, and carry our crosses lovingly, the graces that stem from them are inestimable, not only for us personally, but for their redemptrice repercussions through all humankind, because it is Christ in you and in me who is suffering and carry your cross and my cross – his cross.

The meeting of Jesus with his mother while he was carrying the cross is not mentioned in the Gospels. It may or it may not have taken place. But, as we have seen, Mary was not far away, though it is very unlikely that she and Jesus were able to speak to one another at any time. That is to say, they didn't speak with words, but words aren't always necessary for communication.

What is absolutely sure is that Mary is also very close to us as we make our way through life. As everyone knows, we can't do that without many a cross. We do not see Mary with our human vision, but sight isn't necessary for communication. If we could really believe in our oneness with Christ, really grasp something of what that means, we would be convinced of Mary's interest in us and deep love for us, children of hers, in him.

As we make our way through the ups and downs of life let's look to Mary as our Mother and say: 'Hail Mary, full of grace . . .'

CHAPTER TWENTY-FIVE

The Crucifixion

Imagine that you had never seen a crucifix and that one day you walked into a church and stared up at a large cross and saw, nailed to it, the life-sized figure of a man – dead.

We see a crucifix so often that we become familiar with it. We look at it without seeing. Sometimes a crucifix is used as an ornament, a meaningless object that says nothing to us, and which we do not even treat with respect.

I always find it very difficult to write, or speak, about the crucifixion. Anything that I might say, or write, seems so completely inadequate. 'Jesus died on the cross.' Five simple words, but nothing, in the length and breadth of the whole world's history, is as fraught with significance, vital for every human being born into the world, as these five words, 'Jesus died on the cross.'

God can't die. Jesus died as a man. To die God had to enter creation and assume human nature. Jesus died on the cross, and Jesus was God.

We can't understand God. Death is hard to comprehend. That God should die on a cross is absolutely beyond the scope of our understanding. And yet, this mystery touches the very core of the being of each and every one of us. For Jesus died in my place and yours. Jesus yielded up his human life so that humankind could have a share in his divine life. Human life is something we know, though we are unable to unravel all its mysteries, how then can we begin to grasp the meaning of divine life? We can't.

I am not going to attempt to describe, step-by-step, the terrible fact of the physical crucifixion of the man-God. It was one of the cruellest forms of execution ever thought up, and was reserved for criminals and slaves. Jesus was neither. We, however, were caught up in the slavery brought about by the wicked folly of our kind, a folly and sinfulness to which we all too often give our assent. We were born into this mess; it is our condition and we couldn't get out of it even if we wanted to. All too often we prefer to stay in it, and add by our own sinfulness to the load of human guilt.

God loves us too much to leave us like this. But humanity had to pay a price to be rescued from this human-made mire, and humanity had not the wherewithal to pay. Only God could do this, yet humankind owed the debt, and humankind must pay. God assumed humanity, God became a man in the person of Jesus, and Jesus who was God as well as man, paid in the name of all humanity.

Jesus was no whipping boy taking the punishment instead of us. If that had been the case justice would not have been done and we wouldn't have been helped. No, he was *us*. As long as we remain united to him we can be sure that, in him, we died, and with him, we will rise again to the eternal happiness of the Love-life of the Trinity.

No-one was ever so united to Jesus as was Mary, and no-one so surely died in him as she did standing there, at the foot of the cross during those three long hours of agony.

Let's turn to Mary, the mother of Sorrows, Jesus' mother and ours, with her let us love Jesus with all our hearts, and thank him for rescuing us from sin, and let us say: 'Hail Mary, full of grace . . .'

The Glorious Mysteries

CHAPTER TWENTY-SIX

The Resurrection

They rolled the stone in front of the tomb and sealed it securely. And Mary, what did she do? We don't really know. Perhaps she stood looking at the tomb with unseeing eyes and a strange peace in her heart until John gently led her away.

Mary knew Jesus better than anyone else did, and she understood better than the others what the events of those few days were all about. She did not see the tomb, she saw beyond it. Jesus had said to the disciples; 'The Son of Man will be delivered into the hands of men; they will put him to death; and three days after he has been put to death he will rise again.' The evangelist adds: 'But they did not understand what he said and were afraid to ask him' (Mark 9:31–32). Mary had always 'pondered in her heart' the words of her son, and even if she didn't fully understand, she always believed and trusted. So she knew now that his sufferings were over and in three days he would rise again. She was at peace.

We don't understand the Resurrection either. We just know that Jesus did rise again, and the 'how' of it puzzles us a little. We know that after he had risen he was really alive, but there was something different: his life had taken on new dimensions and shed our human limitations. At one time he was visible, at another he couldn't be seen, he just came and went as he pleased. He walked through walls and doors as if they weren't there, and yet he was a real man. To prove this he invited the disciples to touch him, and asked for food and ate it in front of them, and then he disappeared.

Then there was that strange phenomenon of people seeing

him and speaking to him without recognizing him, until he gave some sign, and suddenly they knew who he was. In the garden Mary Magdalene thought he was the gardener, on the road to Emmaus the two disciples took him for a stranger, they invited him in and at the 'breaking of bread', 'their eyes were opened and they recognized him' (Luke 24:31).

He was alive again, that was sure, but although he was in this world, he was also living in another sphere, the sphere of eternity. He was alive, more alive than ever, now even his human nature was glorified. He had passed through the gates of death and, triumphant, he could suffer and die no more. In the higher, eternal life, to which he had risen, he was no longer fettered by time and place but was completely free.

At last Jesus had come into his own and his Kingdom was established. And where he went we are to follow. We couldn't have followed if he hadn't gone on before. The Crucifixion was not the end, eternal life in the Kingdom followed, and the ignominious crown of thorns became a crown of glory.

We too must suffer and die, but it is not the end for us either! The wonderful thing about the Resurrection is that it gives us a glimpse of what is waiting for us: perfect happiness in the freedom of children of God in the eternal Kingdom. The ordinary way of getting our entrance ticket even now, is by baptism: 'You have been taught that when we were baptised in Christ Jesus we were baptised in his death; in other words, when we were baptised we went into the tomb with him and joined him in death, so that as Christ was raised from the dead by the Father's glory, we too might live a new life' (Romans 6:3–4).

He was the first, but as we are one with him, we are to follow. And surely the one of us who followed him most closely was his mother, Mary. Let us rejoice with her and congratulate her as we say: 'Hail Mary, full of grace ...'

CHAPTER TWENTY-SEVEN

The Ascension

The Scriptures tell us that 'he was lifted up, while they looked on, and a cloud took him from their sight' (Acts 1:9). That is something really extraordinary! It certainly happened as St Luke describes it, but what then? Where did Jesus go when that cloud took him away? The disciples kept on 'staring into the sky' (Acts 1:10) but they could not see Jesus any more.

St Luke also tells us that 'he was withdrawn from them and carried up to Heaven' (Luke 24:51). That rather sounds as if Heaven were somewhere up in space like another planet. St Luke's difficulty, like ours, is that he was talking about divine things and only had human language to do it with. Heaven isn't a material place like Mars or Jupiter, one that we can situate or measure. Heaven is quite simply where God is, and God is everywhere. God is transcendent, that is, out and beyond all or understanding. In that sense we can say God is *up there*.

Jesus is God, God with a human nature, and now the human nature, the *man* Jesus has been glorified and united to the Trinity for all eternity. We don't really know what it means to say that a body has been glorified, we find it hard to imagine what the next world will be like. We just know that a glorified body is no longer limited by time and place, like we are. But, glorified or not, Jesus is the same person, the same Jesus.

We don't understand how God is everywhere so we can't explain how Jesus is everywhere, that is to say, not in the transcendent sense. But there are two other ways in which Jesus is everywhere and these he has pointed out to us.

First, he is really and truly present, body and soul, humanity and divinity, in the Blessed Sacrament. The altar bread and the wine in the chalice are transformed into Jesus, really present, every time a priest consecrates them at Holy Mass. 'This is my body, this is my blood,' Jesus said at the Last Supper, and added, 'Do this as a memorial of me' (Luke 22:19). And that happens all over the world, openly or in secret, under every possible sky. No wonder the 'men in white' asked the disciples why they were looking up into the sky (Acts 1:11). Jesus can't be found that way. He is in Heaven, but Heaven can be on earth, everywhere where there's a consecrated Host.

Second, Jesus is present in ourselves as we are one with him. We can find him within ourselves and in each other. Jesus implied this when he said: 'In so far as you did this to one of the least of these brothers of mine, you did it to me' (Matthew 25:40). No-one is excluded from this oneness with Jesus, not even the least.

So although Jesus withdrew from his disciples – that is he withdrew from the mortal lifestyle we lead here on earth – still he kept his promise that he would not leave us orphans, but would be with us till the end of the world (Matthew 28:20). Also he promised: 'I shall return to take you with me so that where I am you may be too' (John 14:3). While awaiting that wonderful day let's turn to Mary who already knows that happiness, and say: 'Hail Mary full of grace . . .'

CHAPTER TWENTY-EIGHT

The Descent of the Holy Spirit

W hen the wind blows it often disturbs some people, upsets them pretty badly in fact. Wind is an extraordinary force, we can't see it but we can feel it all right. We can determine its direction and measure its speed. We can harness it and make it work for us but we can't control it. That is to say, we can't make it come when we want it, change its direction, or make it stop blowing.

Wind may come as a gentle breeze, beautifully refreshing, or it can come as a raging tornado. It can carry pollen from flower to flower or tree to tree, or it can lift roofs off houses. It can disperse pollution, or raise sand storms. It can bring longed for rain clouds, or destroy forests. Wind is an ordinary, physical force that we all recognize and take for granted, but it so lends itself to powerful symbolism that it is no wonder that God the Holy Spirit choose it as a sign of divine presence.

The disciples, and Mary (she was specifically mentioned as being among them) were all gathered together in a house in Jerusalem. They were very shaken by all events of the past few weeks, uncertain as to what would happen next, and rather afraid of the Jews. They did the wise thing: they turned to God, 'All joined in continuous prayer' (Acts 1:14).

They were still living like this ten days after the Ascension of Jesus when, one day, the whole house was suddenly filled with the sound of a great wind. The Holy Spirit had come among them with power. Then 'tongues of fire' appeared and seemed to rest on the heads of everyone present. St Luke adds; 'They were all filled with the Holy Spirit' (Acts 2:1-4).

St Luke goes on to say that they all started speaking, or being understood, in foreign languages. There were a lot of foreigners in Jerusalem for the feast, and they all understood what was being said in their own languages. St Peter made a speech to those outside the house, and there seems to have been quite a crowd, about three thousand of them were converted to faith in Jesus. From then on the disciples grew brave and fearless and boldly preached everywhere that Jesus was the Son of God and had risen from the dead.

All that was terrific, but we'd love to know what it really felt like being in that room that day. We can only surmise. In any case everybody was probably behaving rather unusually because the people outside thought that they were drunk! Were they so excited, happy and carried away that they hardly knew what they were doing?

We have been so brought up to think of some kinds of behaviour as unacceptable, in particular we have been so conditioned to decorous comportment in church, that conduct that is in any way unrestrained, especially at religious gatherings, tends to be frowned upon. We even occasionally meet a few people who still disapprove of folk music in church. Yet here we have a situation on that first Pentecost day where everyone seems to have been nearly delirious with joy!

Even the combination of the two symbols, wind and fire, would suggest the breaking down of old, rigid, repressive structures and the beginning of a new era of freedom in God. Not licentiousness, but a liberty to use every fibre and faculty in the worship, as well as the service, of God. We are free beings, free with the freedom of the children of God, and there is no harm in some of this being manifested in our religious celebrations.

We are God's children, and as such we are filled with the Holy Spirit. All sin and selfishness, therefore, should be blown away, and zeal for the Kingdom of God should be burning brightly in us, and every bit of our being straining towards the building up of that Kingdom.

Mary had always enjoyed this freedom; I think she must have

been a totally relaxed person. The Holy Spirit was certainly no stranger to her. She had conceived by the power of the Spirit, and by the Spirit she was certainly led and guided all through her earthly life. Now, united to the Spirit in eternal bliss and glory, she is our advocate and protector. So let's sing to her trustfully and joyously saying: 'Hail Mary, full of grace ...'

CHAPTER TWENTY-NINE

The Assumption

The Church believes that Mary 'at the end of the course of her earthly life was raised with her body and soul to Heavenly glory'.[14]

What exactly does that mean? All we can say is that this is part of 'the things that no eye has seen and no ear heard, things beyond the mind of man, all that God has prepared for those who love him' (1 Corinthians 2:9). Very, very little has been revealed about life after death. Jesus' Resurrection and risen life until the Ascension lift just a corner of the curtain and are proof that there is an after-life. The rest we must take on faith, and look forward to a marvellous surprise!

So we don't really know what happened at Mary's assumption other than that her body did not remain to corrupt in the tomb but was raised up again and reunited to her soul. She was taken out of the sight of those around her and united to her son – in Heaven. Heaven is not a geographically locatable, material place, so when we talk of it, or what goes on there, we are just babbling with our human words about matters beyond our ken.

If we can't explain the 'how' of the Assumption, we find it just a little easier to discuss the 'why'. We know that we also shall rise from the grave; Mary's resurrection was immediate, we must wait for ours, and that because of our sinfulness. In any case it is a magnificent destiny that awaits us, immeasurably above anything natural to our human existence.

I wonder, do we instinctively sense that we were born to be something higher, something better than we actually are? Perhaps a misconception of this is behind all our pride and ambition, all our uppishness. The trouble is that we set our sights on the wrong goals, we think we can raise ourselves by our own efforts and merits, and consider promotion and betterment to be our due. We never completely get rid of this pride.

We *are* destined for greatness and glory beyond our wildest imagining, but this is God's doing, God's gift to us, we are for nothing in it, nothing at all, and that is what our pride can't accept. To admit our total nothingness seems like a contradiction denying our destiny. This pride fills us so full of trash that there is no room for grace, that is to say, the gifts that God is so anxious to bestow on us.

Before we can enter the glory of Christ we must die. Not only die, but everything that is 'us', even our mortal bodies, must totally perish. Disintegration after death is the final blow to human pride. After that will come the resurrection of our bodies, which is God's work!

Mary was sinless, so Mary was free from pride. She didn't deny the gifts God gave her, but she recognized them as gifts. 'From this day forward all generations will call me blessed,' she said, 'for the Almighty has done great things for me' (Luke 1:48–49). As her humility was perfect God could fill her as no other human being has ever been filled, she became pregnant with God, and gave birth to a child who was God.

There was no need therefore for her body to disintegrate. Not only no need, but it would have been unfitting for a body that had been so closely associated with divinity to disintegrate. So Mary was raised body and soul to Heavenly glory.

No-one saw it happen. Tradition has it that after her death, some disciples who had travelled from a distance, arrived too late for the burial. They wanted to look upon Mary's features once again so the tomb was re-opened. It was found to be empty. This is only a tradition and is unimportant. It is the fact of the Assumption that matters and the Church has always held to that belief.

We accept that the bodies of both Jesus and Mary are now spiritual, glorified. What that really means we don't know but they are real bodies all the same. We believe also that we too shall be glorified one day. While waiting for that happy day let's congratulate Mary, and rejoice with her as we say: 'Hail Mary, full of grace ...'

CHAPTER THIRTY

The Coronation of Mary

Of course this didn't really happen at all. There aren't any crowns in heaven, nor thrones, nor harps, any more than angels have wings or saints wear haloes. Our human language is so limited when it comes to talking about divine things that we are obliged to use symbols to express ourselves. The danger is that we take the symbols literally and then say: 'No, this just isn't possible!'

Let us see if we can understand these symbols a little better. What we are trying to do when we use them, is to describe the tremendous happiness, power and glory of Heaven, and, in the case of Mary's coronation, we want to express the wonderful honour and dignity to which Mary has been raised. Actually, for all our talk of thrones and crowns, for all the superlative adjectives I might feel obliged to pile up in my effort to describe the honour paid to Mary, we can only fall terribly short of the reality!

Our words are like those spectacular firework shows people put on when they want to celebrate. When all is said and done they are just a few bangs and a brief appearance of coloured stars that die as soon as they are born. Even the most fantastic firework show pales before God's handiwork. Think, for example, of some of those magnificent sunsets we often see, or the thrilling awesomeness of a thunderstorm with lightning flashing. God has certainly more resources than we have, and the demonstration of God's beauty and power, that we see in our skies, is only the edge of the fringe of God's real strength and magnificence. So what must the welcome Mary received in Heaven been like!

Mary is like a queen in Heaven. No, she is Queen of Heaven! So great was her role on earth of giving birth to God's son, so rich was her response to God's grace, so humbly did she attribute everything to God, that now her glory and happiness are immeasurable and inexpressible. The best we can do to express this is to say that she has been crowned queen. With our limited speech we can't say more, but we can ponder the greatness and glory of Mary as we meditate this fifth glorious mystery of her rosary.

But we must never, never fall into the error of thinking that because Mary is now so great, she has been distanced from us. No, that is not so. She is always one of us, the first of us, the queen of us, yes, but she is also the mother of us. Mary our mother! She knows full well that her glory is not from herself but from God. She is not surrounded by protocol or body-guards. She hasn't forgotten the poverty of Bethlehem, the hardships of Egypt, the streets of Jerusalem, not the pain of the cross. So she is accessible to all of us, and approachable even to the littlest or the worst of us. She understands, and she loves us.

Because Mary is now glorified she has, as I have already said, the qualities of a glorified body, so she is not bound by time and space. That means that whoever we are, wherever we are, she can be present to us, she can listen to us and she can help us. Walls and doors are not barriers for her, neither do miles or years cause any problems, she is in full control, Queen of Heaven and Queen of the Universe! In a vision to St Catherine Laboure, Mary complained that people don't ask for the graces of which her hands are so full. Of course if we doubt her power, or don't trust her, we put obstacles in the way of those graces. Let's make sure that Mary is really the queen of each of us as we praise her with songs of love and say: 'Hail Mary, full of grace ...'

Postscript

The Angelus

Victoria Street was as full and busy as usual as I made my way to the Underground. It was about mid-day, but I hadn't averted to the fact until the Cathedral bell rang out three strokes. No-one stopped or looked up, everyone just continued on their way.

'The Angel of the Lord declared unto Mary,' I said under my breath, 'and she conceived of the Holy Spirit.' That really was putting it in a nutshell! The great drama of the incarnation summed up in two sentences. I conjured up the scene in my mind: Mary mysteriously invited to divine motherhood!

'Hail Mary,' the Angel had said. I repeated the words saying the lovely little prayer we know so well. The bell rang out again. 'Behold the handmaid of the Lord,' I whispered, 'be it done unto me according to thy word.' That was the way Mary expressed her total availability, the availability of one who belonged completely to God.

'Hail Mary,' I said again, praying that I might emulate Mary's availability, if only just a little.

Once more the bell rang out. 'And the Word was made flesh,' I said, reflecting on the awesomeness of the mystery of God assuming our humanity, 'and dwelt amongst us.' The crowd was milling past. How many of these people of every race and every creed, or no creed at all, knew that God was among them?

'Hail Mary,' I murmured, 'pray for us sinners' who turn away, not recognizing God's loving presence among us, 'Yes, Mary, pray for us, Oh holy Mother of God, that we may be made worthy of the promises of Christ.'

Then, turning to God, I prayed that as we know about Mary

becoming Mother of God, we may also share in the glory and happiness her son won for us by his death and rising again. 'Pour forth, we beseech thee, O Lord, thy grace into our hearts, that we to whom the Incarnation of Christ thy Son was made known by the message of an angel, may by his passion and death be brought to the glory of his resurrection, through Christ, our Lord, Amen.'

The bell had stopped ringing. The crowds were still milling by and I passed on my way, my heart lightened and refreshed by this little rendezvous with Mary in the middle of Victoria Street! No-one about me knew anything about it. Neither did I know what passed within the secret realm of the souls of those about me. Perhaps many of those passing by had also said the Angelus, perhaps dozens and dozens had joined in me that meeting with Mary. And in other parts of London other church bells also rang out the Angelus, and in other parts of the country too.

The Angelus! That beautiful old custom lives on, just a short prayer greeting Mary as the Angel greeted her long ago, revering her as the virgin mother of Jesus, God and man. Many of us greet Mary like this three times a day, in the early morning, at mid-day and again in the evening. Even if we say this prayer only once a day, it helps to keep us in touch with Mary and Jesus and keeps us close to them. It also brings down many blessings upon us and for those for whom we pray.

Just a little prayer but so fraught with meaning!

Source Notes

1. 'The Wonders He Has Done For You', *Eagle's Wings*. Anthology of verse in the series *Scripture in Song*, Chevalier Press, P.O. Box 13, Kensington, NSW, Australia.

2. *Redemptoris Mater*, Pope John Paul II.

3. 'Adam', *Dictionary of Biblical Theology*, Xavier Leon-Dufour.

4. *Ineffabilis*.

5. *RSV*.

6. In the *RSV* edition the word 'slave' is given as 'servant'.

7. *RSV*.

8. *Mary Mother of the Lord*, Karl Rahner, Anthony Clarke Books.

9. *Ibid*.

10. *Ibid*.

11. *RSV*.

12. St Bernard, quoted in *Redemptoris Mater*, Pope John Paul II.

13. *Mary Mother of the Lord*, Karl Rahner, Anthony Clarke Books.

14. *Urbi et Orbi*, Pius XII.

Source Notes